MEETING JESUS IN THE HOLY LAND

IGNATIUS FERNANDEZ

Copyright © Ignatius Fernandez
All Rights Reserved.

This book is dedicated to the unsung heroes of the Holy Land – the monks, priests, pastors, brothers, nuns, and lay people who work tirelessly to keep the place in readiness for visitors, who come and go. These heroes stay on to welcome the next group. And, to my sons who sponsored me for the tour.

Contents

Foreword

Mr. Fernandez, quite exceptionally, has not just managed to sustain the intensity of his enriching experience during his pilgrimage but also has successfully transformed it into a labor of love – the book you are reading.

Fr. S Devadass SVD,Parish Priest, Saint Alphonsa Church, Hyderabad, India.

For the wealth of information that one gleans from its pages, this is a must-read. If one plans a visit to the Holy Land, this book is indispensable.

Rex D'Silva,Former Data-System Engineer with Siemens and Philips in Europe and the Middle East, Trivandrum, India.

Each biblical site is organized according to scriptural background, archaeological history, reflections on sites and happenings (this is where the book shines), to shed light on our spiritual lives.

Francis J Irudairaj, Assistant Vice President (Human Resources), Kuwait Financial Center, and author of Re-engineering Readiness, Kuwait.

The book is far more than a travelogue: it offers excellent material for spiritual reading that can inspire and challenge the reader. The reading public has a good reason to be thankful to the author for this gift.

Fr. George Kaitholil ssp, Former General Editor of Saint Pauls and Better Yours Books, and prolific author of ninety two books.

The author has very detailed descriptions of the various sites, with historical facts, to give the reader a better understanding of many facets of Christianity.

Elwyn Netto, Former Director HRC, Kanan Devan Hills Plantation (Tata Tea), Alwaye, Kerala, India.

Meeting Jesus in the Holy Land is the author's tenth book. As with his previous books, his down-to-earth, reflective, and non-preachy writing comes to the fore. He does not depend on visual crutches but through words paints a picture in the reader's mind, of each of the places he visits in the Holy Land.

Joseph Rozario, Marketing Communications Specialist, Chennai, India.

The book is a fascinating mix of Biblical and modern-day history, travel to the Holy Land, and a call to spiritual reflection. Only Ignatius can mix these ingredients in an engaging narrative, that had me wishing that the book was longer!

Edward Valenzuela, Former Managing Director, Accenture LLC, Colorado, USA.

Preface

PREFACE

The purpose of a pilgrimage in the Christian Tradition is 'transformation', a complete metamorphosis of the individual's identity, vision and mission. This was documented by the Scripture Writer, and confirmed by theologians, in the recorded pilgrimage of an Ethiopian to Jerusalem when he met the apostle Philip. (Acts. 8:26-40). This pilgrim was baptized and given the gift of evangelism.

It is not that Mr. Fernandez did not possess the gift of evangelizing and sharing Christocentric experiences with others, before his pilgrimage to the Holy Land. Rather, his zeal to share Christ became more intense after his visit to the Holy Land. Few of us, after experiencing an emotionally intense encounter, are able to configure it into an instrument of witness and sharing. Mr. Fernandez, quite exceptionally, has not just managed to sustain the intensity of his enriching experience in the Holy Land but also transform it successfully into a 'labour of love,' – the book you are reading now!

Now travels are synonymous with journeys undertaken to admire human achievements – architecture, pleasure spots and adventure. However, the book on a pilgrimage, "MEETING JESUS IN THE HOLY LAND" serves a different purpose. It nudges the reader to discover the sacred element in geographical sites. Doing a fabulous job, the author unveils what is special at each location, as a lover of Jesus would want. Traversing the Old and New Testaments, the book dwells on lessons the visitor might learn on the visit to the Holy Land. Kudos to the author for not playing the role of a tourist guide, but of a zealous Christian, vouching for the fact that God did walk this earth!

I am delighted that he was a part of the group from this parish, that made the tour.

With Prayerful wishes,

Fr. S. Devadass, SVD,

Parish Priest, St. Alphonsa Church, Hyderabad, India.

Acknowledgements

Neil Armstrong – the first man to land on the moon – was on a tour of the Holy Land, after the lunar mission. He was accompanied by Meir Ben-Dov, the Israeli archaeologist. At the steps leading to the Temple, Armstrong asked Meir if Jesus had climbed those steps. The archaeologist gave him a positive response. Immediately Armstrong proclaimed: *"I have to tell you, I am more excited stepping on these stones, than I was stepping on the moon."* I did not set foot on the moon, but I can tell you that I was more excited walking the Holy Land, where Jesus walked, than when my first book was published.

My sons made the visit possible by sponsoring me. I thank them for their generosity, and thoughtfulness.

This book would not have been written, but for the enlightenment and Mercy of the **Holy Spirit**. His support was miraculous! I kneel in gratitude.

I thank Father S Devadass for writing an engaging Preface – despite his travel out of town for a long retreat. His going into depth, has brought to the surface thoughts concealed under pages of prose.

The reviewers have done a masterful analysis of the book, to highlight thoughts that struck them. They too worked against constraints to fulfill their commitment to me - in elegant language that captures the essence of the book, and to give readers an overview.

My grandson, Marcus Ignatius Fernandez, helped me post the cover picture and the twelve in the book. I thank him warmly.

And I thank you – readers – for studying this book to help you refresh memories of the tour you made some time ago, or as a preparation for the tour you plan to make.

The Bible comes alive in the Holy Land, that Fathers of the Church have called it the fifth Gospel. May The Lord be with you as you read of the fifth Gospel, and bless you abundantly!

Ignatius Fernandez.

www.ignatiusfernandez.com

The Tour

Chapter one: The Tour

"Our hearts were made for you, O God, and they shall not rest until they rest in you." Saint Augustine

Caution: This is not a book of fiction, which will thrill you as you turn pages to discover twists in the plot, bold moves of the hero or the dark deeds of the villain. It is a book of nonfiction, with JESUS as the larger-than-life central figure - the thorn-pierced King; not the king born in a palace, but in a cave. Not the popular hero who is feted, but the adversary of the Jewish elders, who plot to kill him. He owns nothing and does not claim the high seat. He gave up everything to give us everything!

So, let us read it with attention and prayer; not to be entertained, but edified by thoughts on the sterling life of Jesus - our Lord and Master. Since we undertake this tour as sinners, bent on changing our ways, I try to introduce some reflection, where possible, in the hope that we turn inward, even as we ponder the sites we visit. *"The longest journey is the journey inward"* Dag Hammarsjold.

Let us visit the places where our Lord walked, talked and performed. Let us make the tour of the Holy Land (notice that there is no other land with the prefix *"holy"*) through pages of this book, to carry with us images that will outlast the pictures we take with our smart phones or cameras. Let us treasure those visuals in the deep recesses of our minds to make JESUS the only reason we live.

A dream come true: From my youth I hoped to visit the Holy Land. Time and age tip-toed past me, but my dream remained so until 2017, when I joined a group of 28, to make the tour – thanks to my sons who sponsored me. James Sylvester and Father Satish Banda of Saint Alphonsa Parish, Hyderabad, India, organized the tour, which they did splendidly. To state that it was a dream come true would be an understatement – because it shook me to my roots. It was a transforming experience that I find difficult to put into words. Many on the tour agreed that the tour was life-changing. As you read, please pause to take in the sanctity of each site and marvel at the wonders the Lord did – for us; for you and for me.

Four countries: We covered four countries – Jordan, Israel, Palestine and Egypt - in ten days. Exhausting, but exhilarating! Bahrain was the first stop. From there we flew to Amman, the capital of Jordan. For the next ten days we travelled by air-conditioned bus to visit sites in the Holy Land. From Cairo, in Egypt, we returned home.

This book is not a travelogue on the Holy Land – giving you a sequential account of sights, sounds and smells on the tour; not a description of the miles we travelled from country to country, but of the miles we travelled inward, in a spiritual discovery. Join me on a journey of faith, with Scripture as a guide.

Jordan: It is an Arab nation on the east bank of the Jordan River. It is endowed with ancient monuments, nature reserves and seaside resorts. It is home to the famed archaeological site of Petra – Rose City – going back to 300 BC. Jordan is bordered by Saudi Arabia to the South, Iraq to the north-east, Syria to the north and Israel/Palestine to the west. The Dead Sea is located along its western borders, and it has a small coastline with the Red Sea, to the south-west. It is the founding member of the Arab League. Wisely, she has welcomed refugees and promoted medical tourism.

It is a kingdom of about 10 million people, where the king wields power, unlike the UK where the King/Queen is a ceremonial head. Of the population, 95% is Muslim and 5% Christian. Amman, the capital, is broadly divided into the modern west, and the traditional east. On red soil, olive and fig-farms are plenty. The land does not produce oil, but yields minerals, which promote brisk trade. Construction follows the Arabic Style, with prominent pillars in the front of such buildings. Mostly houses are small; a few big ones dot the landscape. There are only a few malls and not many shops. Like the three other countries, cars motor on the right side of fairly well-maintained roads (American style). In Jordan, besides the holy sites, we did not visit tourist spots.

Palestine: It is our next stop. It is a de jure sovereign state in Western-Asia – claiming the West Bank and the Gaza Strip. Ramallah is its administrative center. It is recognized by 136 UN members. Of its population of about 5 million, 93% are Muslims and about 6% Christian. Narrow streets, congested traffic and a run-down appearance, stamp the place. Tension is palpable – with occasional skirmishes between Palestine and Israel, although major conflicts are kept in check because of the superior muscle power that Israel exercises. Arabic is the language commonly spoken, although English is spoken among people of the upper class.

Houses are small and found in clusters. Only a few big buildings stand out, with shops scattered among them. Bargaining is the way business is conducted, so tourists tend to buy things in Palestine, where they are cheaper. In this region, we did not visit tourist spots, only holy sites.

Israel: With Lebanon to the north, Syria to the north-east, Jordan to the east, Palestine to the east and west, and Egypt to the south west, Israel is hedged in by strong neighbors who do not relish the progress she has made. A short fuse burns, threatening an explosion and an end to a fragile peace. At first Egypt held Jews captive. Moses led them home under God's guiding hand. Then the Assyrians captured the land. Babylon overran Assyria and they became the new masters. Persia defeated Babylon and Cyrus gave Israel its long lost freedom. Then Rome took over. Rome subjugated the area for more than 60 years before the birth of Jesus. Therefore, Roman influence was apparent at the time Jesus lived. Although Latin is not spoken now, books in Latin have enriched the literature of the region. Currently, Hebrew and Arabic are the official languages; but English is popular among the upper class.

Israel is relatively small, with a population of about 9 million; one of the smaller states in India boasts of a higher population. Though small, she is neat and tidy. Because of her size and the rich lifestyle of her people, traffic jams are common. The rich have their homes on high-priced hill tops, while the middle-class and the poor live on the plains. Even in Tel Aviv, high-rise buildings are not many. But she is prolific in building and maintaining museums – per capita more than any other country in the world. Tel Aviv, the capital until recently, is known for its Bauhaus Architecture (bridging art and industry, which originated in Germany), and splendid beaches. Passing Haifa, Israel's largest port, gives us a glimpse of the brisk business she does with the world, even from her narrow borders.

Her determination to excel is seen in the way she defends herself against many and powerful neighbors, resulting in a state of perpetual preparedness, and increasing defence expenditure. Besides threats from outside, she is alert to trouble that Palestine can trigger. The Economist (an internationally popular magazine) of February 2-8, 2019, provides some information on the changing scene. Among 200,000 Arabs, 500 Jews live in the old town of Hebron – where the tension is palpable. In East Jerusalem 220,000 Jews live among 345,000 Arabs. The growing number of Arabs, in a tenuous truce, is worrisome to the Jews. By extending settlements and erecting more barricades for Palestinians, the Jews have not made things easier for themselves. The Palestinian Authority, in the West Bank, and Hamas, its Islamic rival, watch things closely only to pounce on their strong neighbour, when conditions favourable to them prevail. Israel has not known peace since her formation in 1948, and is not likely to know of it in the near future.

The way the Jews have innovated is seen in the many developments they have engineered. What struck us was the way they manage water – a scarce resource. The River Jordan is the main source of fresh water. Not to be heavily dependent on it, they desalinate sea water to meet about two-thirds of their water needs. They recycle sewage water to reduce about 10% of the deficit. And, through drip irrigation, they save about 15-20%. Literally, the desert blooms with flowers, fruits, rice and barley.

Visiting Israel makes the Holy Bible come alive, even as dates that drip a sugary liquid remind us of the land of milk and honey that the God gave Abraham.

Egypt: It connects north-east Africa with the Middle-East. Bordered by the Gaza Strip and Israel to the north-east, the Gulf of Aqaba to the east, the Red Sea to the east and south, Sudan to the south, and Libya to the west, this Mediterranean country has a long history; like India. Islam is the official religion and Arabic the official language – for a population of 95 million.

After a long bus-ride we reach Cairo, the capital of Egypt. A cruise on the river Nile, as the boat hugs the shore, gives us a glimpse of the night life in Cairo. On the boat, we are entertained to Arabic songs and belly-dancing. Over two hours on the boat and a leisurely dinner, we take in the beauty of the Nile. It is difficult to visualize Egypt without the Nile, which is the main source of water, for a rain-deprived country. No industrial waste is allowed into the river, to leave it relatively clean. It starts in Burundi, in Africa, flows through some other African countries, and through Egypt, before it empties itself into the Mediterranean Sea. Of its total length of 6,800 kilometers, 1200 flow through Egypt. Its majestic flow is interrupted by tiny islands that lend it a fairyland appearance.

Cairo has a population of about 20 million. It is dirty, dusty and busy like any of the major cities in India - Mumbai, Kolkata, or Delhi.

Travel: We were fortunate to have guides at the four places who were informed, polite, helpful and articulate. They answered questions and clarified doubts. They stepped out of their professional boundaries to help us, when we needed help. The air-conditioned buses in which we traveled, were swift, clean and fairly quiet.

The weather, at the start of spring, in late February/ early March, was pleasant. Light warm clothing was adequate. The time difference with India , for the four countries, is about three-and-a-half hours: 10 a.m. in India is 6.30 a.m. local time.

In retrospect, the tour was enriching, but tiring. Strong legs to walk long distances and climb steep gradients helped us. But a strong and determined mind made all the difference. Teresa Smith (84) was our inspiration. Despite her aching knees, she did not stop, but plodded on, to our amazement. A remarkable lady!

Jesus inspired the people of his time. Doubtless, he will take us into his huge embrace. It is from the Holy Land that his word spread to four corners of the world. The grains of sand on which he walked are charged with memories and the power to transform us. May the earthly Holy Land that does not last forever, lead us to the heavenly holy land that lasts forever!

I hope you keep me close company, as we travel from site to site, keeping the image of Jesus before us. A few pictures, taken by me, are spread across this book, to keep alive memories of the Holy Land.

CHAPTER TWO

The Holy Land

"It is for the sake of man, not God, that worship and prayers are required, not that God may be rendered more glorious, but that man may be made better." Hugh Blair

The Holy Land is the area located between the Jordan River and the Mediterranean Sea, that includes the Eastern Bank of the river. Traditionally, it is synonymous with the Biblical land of Israel, Palestine, Western Jordan, Parts of Lebanon, and parts of Southern Syria. It is considered to be holy by Jews, Christians and Muslims as seen in the Old Testament, the New Testament and the Koran.

The sanctity of the land to the Christians led to the war of the Crusades, when they tried to wrench it from the Muslims, who had captured it from Byzantine Europe. Therefore, it was no exaggeration when the Synod Fathers referred to the Holy Land as the "fifth Gospel". To realize the significance of the Fifth Gospel, it is right that we immerse ourselves in the four Gospels, to spot the continuation found in the fifth. In our narration, we shall keep the Gospel of Matthew as a signpost for sequence and substance. Where necessary, we shall switch to the other Gospels, to ensure that the thread is not cut. For sites of the Old Testament, Genesis is the beginning.

Part of the Holy Land is fertile, part desert. Scars of battles, fires, and earthquakes mark the land. At different times, Persians, Turks and other Muslims ravaged the place. They reduced churches to rubble, but reconstruction restored the original in a way, with notable additions. Today it is home to a mix of people – Jews, Muslims, Christians, Bedouin and others. Despite being arid in places, it is blessed by Nature – stately mountains, secret tunnels, meandering rivers, ascending and descending terrain and lush foliage. It is a place that is steeped in history – where rocks have silently witnessed thousands of events that have shaped and reshaped the face of the land.

The Holy Land is a hive of archaeological activity. So much of history lies buried beneath rock and sand, that it takes diligent work by committed archeologists to uncover secrets hidden below the earth. One such project is the reconstructing of the Umm el-Kanatir synagogue, on the Golan Heights, devastated by an earthquake in 749 AD. It was the oldest in Gamla. Using 21st century technology, Yeshu Dray and his team have put back a good part of the synagogue, to the astonishment of visitors. As you move around the Holy Land, chances are that you will see more such restoration work.

When you traverse the paths that Jesus trod, some that Moses and David walked, be prepared to be awed at the spots that commemorate the Beatitudes, the Lord's Prayer, the raising of Lazarus from the dead, the Transfiguration, the Last Supper, the trial of Jesus, his crucifixion and resurrection; also spots hallowed by Old Testament heroes. Stand by and admire the bronze snake that Moses shaped to heal Jews who were stung by snakes in the desert. And, be impressed by the bronze-painted statue of David with his lyre.

When you touch the Wailing Wall, go back in history to the Temple Solomon built – his masterpiece. Over the years the Temple was destroyed by enemies of Israel and rebuilt by the Jews. As Jesus prophesied forty years earlier, no stone on stone was left of the temple, when the Romans vanquished Jewish resistance, in 70 AD. What is left is a sad reminder of a turbulent past.

A visit to the Holy Land is an experience of a lifetime. Savor it! To initiate you into the delight of visiting the Holy Land, here is a list of places you ought not to miss.

Bethlehem: Although the town (which means *"house of bread"*) was occupied by Canaanites about 3000 BC, it gained importance only after the birth of Jesus. There is a line of Biblical personalities who are associated with it: Here Rachel, wife of Jacob, died after giving birth to Benjamin, the last of her 12 sons. It is common knowledge that her 12 sons founded the 12 tribes of Israel. Later, Ruth joined her mother-in-law, Naomi, in Bethlehem, to live with her, although she did not belong there. Boaz, a local land-owner, in whose fields Ruth gleaned grain, married her. Obed, the son of this couple, was the father of Jesse – father of David. In this town, Samuel, the prophet, anointed David as the future King of Israel. Centuries later, Joseph, foster-father of Jesus, also belonged here. That is why he had to trudge to it from Nazareth, for the census.

Although Mary was in an advanced stage of pregnancy, she and Joseph had to make the journey of over 130 kilometers, in about four days. Mary sat on a donkey, as Joseph walked alongside. Travel by foot was dangerous – exposed to bandits and wild animals. Therefore, Joseph and Mary could have traveled in a group. Since they had no room in the inn, they found a cave, where Mary gave birth to the King of Kings. Angels appeared to Shepherds who hurried to adore the Infant King. Later, three wise men from afar, came visiting Jesus, freighted with gifts – Gold, frankincense and myrrh. Since the Wise men did not return to King Herod, to give him news of Jesus, in a fit of rage, he ordered the slaughter of infants. Would their blood cancel his embarrassment? The people of Bethlehem nursed a grudge against Jesus because they lost their babies. Herod unleashed terror, but they blamed Jesus. When Jesus grew up and visited the town, his welcome was muted.

Nazareth: It is the highest point in Southern Galilee – about 20 miles east of the Mediterranean Sea, 15 miles west of the Sea of Galilee, and 5 miles west of Mount Tabor. The Hebrew meaning of Nazareth is: watch or guard. Was it the reason Jesus spent 30 years of his life in that town, in the company of Mary and Joseph, watching things happen, and guarding against distractions from his mission? Training as a carpenter, under the guidance of Joseph, he served the people in the region. At that time there were about 200 people in the town; today there are about 60,000 in the same space. Since Jesus grew up in that town, the locals found it difficult to accept him as a preacher, a rabbi, and rejected him, prompting him to state: *"Truly I tell you, no prophet is accepted in the prophet's hometown" Lk. 4: 24.* The people of Nazareth were known to be nonconformists, rebels. Therefore, others figured that Jesus too was a rebel.

The Basilica of the Annunciation is a must-visit, on this tour – there is a picture of it in the collection of pictures that appear in this book. Nearby are the Orthodox church of Saint Gabriel – the one who announced the good news to Mary - the church of Saint Joseph and the Synagogue church. (More information on churches in the Holy Land appears in a separate chapter.)

Capernaum: The town is located on the shore of the Sea of Galilee, a few miles away from Nazareth. Jesus chose to move out of Nazareth, because the people showed no belief in him; also, Capernaum was a bigger town, with travelers criss-crossing the town on their journeys. From there roads led to Damascus and Egypt. Wheat and olives grew in plenty; and, fruit and fish were abundant. People were prosperous.

In one of the synagogues of this town, Jesus performed miracles. A partially restored synagogue lies atop an older structure that Jesus visited. Was it Peter's house? In Mt. 11: 21-24, Jesus passes judgement on the towns of Chorazin, Bethsaida and Capernaum. Despite his many works of wonder, the people of these towns did not repent, calling upon themselves consequences on Judgement Day.

Jerusalem: Jesus was often seen in Jerusalem, the most important city of the land – the most fought over city for over 5000 years. Tragically, it witnessed his persecution and death on the cross in 30 AD. At that time there were about 40,000 people in the city. With visitors in and out, it was a bustling place . The Temple drew many thousands of visitors at festival time and trade was brisk. Today, the population is much more than before, but it is a divided city (4 parts): The North is the Muslim Quarter, the West is the Christian Quarter, the South-West is the Armenian Quarter and the South-East is the Jewish Quarter. With 1200 synagogues, 150 churches, 70 mosques, narrow cobbled streets, undulating terrain, and high walls, the place is packed with people and produces a cacophony that is unsettling to visitors, but music to the locals. It was meant to be a city of peace. Sadly, it has not known any peace with conquest and destruction playing havoc. The American Embassy shifting from Tel Aviv to Jerusalem has added to the unrest.

For Jews, it is the capital of David's Kingdom, which he captured from the Jebusites 1000 years before Jesus was born. That meant that he built the city 3000 years ago, and rested the Ark of the Covenant in it. Before the shift of the Ark, it was housed at Abu Ghosh. Now a Benedictine Monastery marks Abu Ghosh. The elaborate water supply system of that time is a pointer to how well the city was managed by David. The Tower of David is located in this city. The original citizens did not live in what is today the Old City, but on a narrow ridge that descended from the Temple site. Besides his heroic conquests, David is known to have composed many psalms - praising God even in desperate times. Of 150 psalms in the book of psalms, David is credited with composing about half the number. A site marks the tomb of the warrior king, but its authenticity is debated. A statue of him playing the harp is erected outside the tomb. Besides David and Solomon, prophets Isaiah and Jeremiah, and kings Hezekiah and Josiah, walked there. The historicity of the place was affirmed through seals with Biblical names, that were unearthed.

Despite the ruins, Jerusalem has a melancholic beauty, a vestige of the past that boasts a long history. From the start the Jews suffered oppression in one form or other. For more than four hundred years, they heard the hiss and felt the sting of the master's whip in Egypt. Moses led them home (about 1446 BC). They were not free for long. The twelve tribes that David and Solomon united into one kingdom split into ten tribes (Israel) in the North, and two tribes (Judea) in the South. Infighting continued and there was never peace for any length of time. About 743 BC Assyria invaded Israel. About 701 BC, Assyria besieged Jerusalem, and about 586 BC Judea fell to Babylon. But in

539 BC Persia overran Babylon and Cyrus, the Emperor, allowed the Jews to return home. Strangely, they received mercy from a conqueror, as prophesied. Not long after, the Romans became their new masters. The Muslims moved in, temporarily halted by the Crusaders who lost in a fierce battle. Then the marauding Turks took over. Later Hitler extracted a ransom from them. Not until 1948, after the second world war, did Israel regain her homeland – a land soaked in blood, occupied by a troubled people. Since Jerusalem saw the rise of three religions – Judaism, Christianity and Islam, three languages – Hebrew, English and Arabic - are spoken by most people.

For Christians, it is the place where Jesus taught, healed and performed many miracles. Many churches pack their quarter. There are wide and ornate streets in the Jewish quarter of Jerusalem. For Muslims, it is the place from which Mohammad ascended to heaven. Streets in the Muslim Quarter are narrow, noisy, and colorful. The Armenians have their own quarter and try to stay in it.

About 326 AD Saint Helena, mother of Emperor Constantine, planned to build many churches in the region, which she did. We shall learn more on her churches in the section on churches (chapter ten). In 638 AD the Muslims conquered the area and destroyed churches. They built the Dome of Rock over the Temple Site. In 1099 AD the Crusaders regained much of what was lost to the Muslims, only to lose it again to Saladin the conqueror, in 1187 AD. Later the Turks overran the place. Finally, Israel gained control over the city in 1967 – until then Jordan occupied it, after she captured it in 1948.

Model of Ancient Jerusalem: To give visitors a glimpse of what ancient Jerusalem looked like, a model was built. One leaves in awe after the visit. A sound and light show on Jerusalem lends an aura to the Model. The model, spread across 2000 square meters, was built in the 1960s by Hans Kroch, owner of the Holy Land Hotel. Although there is no guarantee that the model is a faithful reflection of Jerusalem in 66 AD, archaeologists were known to work tirelessly to create a worthy reproduction. Their efforts can be sincerely applauded. Visit it and stand in awe!

Old Jerusalem, in 66 AD, before the Roman invasion in 70 AD, was spread over 180 hectares, more than twice the size of the city, as it stands now. Christianity was still in its infancy – 36 years after Jesus died – and the Dead Sea Scrolls were still being written. Jesus' warning and his tears over Jerusalem foreshadowed events that reduced Jerusalem to rubble.

Temple Mount: It is now just a massive masonry platform that is revered by Jews, Christians and Muslims. They all regard it as the place where Mount Moriah once stood. For Jews, Scripture reminds them that Abraham, on that mountain, was to slay his son Isaac, in obedience to God's command. It is also the place where the Temple stood. For Christians, it is the Temple where Jesus was presented as a baby, in the presence of the holy and wise Simeon and Anna - who prophesied on him. It was also the place where Jesus went when he was 12, to raise and answer questions among the doctors of the law. He was lost and found after three days – prefiguring the time he would be hidden in a tomb. It was the place where Jesus drove out the corrupt traders. Then he addressed the crowds who were waiting to hear from him; soon after he healed many who were ill with one sweep of his hand. All were healed at the same time. It was the place where Jesus shed tears on the fall of Jerusalem and the destruction of the Temple. For Muslims, it is the revered Sanctuary – the third holiest, after Mecca and Medina.

Solomon's Temple, about 740 meters above sea level, was built around 950 BC. It housed the Ark of the Covenant, in which slabs that inscribed the ten commandments, Aaron's staff that flowered, and a sample of manna that God gave the Jews in the desert, were kept. The lavish and huge Temple that Solomon built lasted for about 350 years, until the Babylonians destroyed it. The Jews returned from Babylon about 50 years later, and rebuilt the Temple about 515 BC. Herod the Great rebuilt the Temple in 20 BC. It was 485 meters long on the east, 314 meters on the west, 469 meters on the north and 280 meters on the south. The walls were 50 meters high. With unequal dimensions, it was an irregular structure, that was destroyed by the Romans in 70 AD. Before its fall, in 30 AD, Jesus predicted that no stone would be left on stone.

Saint Helena built a small church at the site of the Temple. In the 7th century, Muslims occupied the land, but were ousted by the Crusaders in 1099 AD. In later years, the Muslims wrenched it from them. At the base of the Temple Mount are the remains of Byzantine monastery, recalling old times. Now, a mosque marks the site, known as the Dome of the Rock. It is revered as the site from which the prophet ascended to heaven.

The Wall: It is the remaining part of the wall that surrounded the Temple, that Herod built in 20 BC. It is 60 feet high and 1500 feet long. It is an unsettling sight, but a place of prayer. Petitions are thrust into clefts in the wall, begging God to hear their prayers. More than a million petitions in a year, in different languages, are ferreted out of their hiding places. Bearded, capped and dressed in blacks, Jews pray at the wall. Their longing for the Temple is visible and painful to watch. For that reason the wall is referred to as the Wailing Wall. The Jews call it KOTEL. The stones that make up the wall are between 2 and 8 tons. The biggest, at the base weighs 570 tons. In awe we wonder at the effort that went into building the wall, more than 2000 years ago. What is left is a sad reminder of what was once a splendid structure! Now three mosques stand in place of the Temple. History reports on the destruction of the Temple, its reconstruction, its destruction once more and another attempt to rebuild, only to suffer again. It seemed that destruction was drawn into its architecture.

In the distant past Jerusalem had eight exit gates, named after places to which the gates led. For example Damascus Gate led to Damascus (recall Saul's conversion on the road to Damascus, to become Paul, the crusader for Christ), Jaffa Gate led to Jaffa and so on.

The praying area at the Wailing Wall is divided into sections for men and women, reminding us of the separate enclosures for men and women, in the Temple of old. Among the more important dignitaries who prayed at the wall, are Pope John Paul II, Pope Benedict XVI, Barrack Obama and Hillary Clinton.

At the left end of the wall is the entrance to a 500-meter long tunnel, that runs under buildings in the old city. With buildings in poor repair, a disaster is waiting to happen.

The Temple that Herod built: Who was Herod who rebuilt the Temple and added to it a tall tower? He was not a King by birth. Part Jew and part Greek he had no right to position, but found favour with the Romans to be put in charge of the territory. Although Rome conquered the Province and controlled it, King Herod was given powers to supervise local matters and settle local disputes, as long as no death penalty was involved. Between 37 and 31 BC,

Herod the Great built the Castle of Masada. Its isolated location and surrounding landscape made attack on it almost impossible. Today, the top of Masada can be reached on foot – an arduous journey, no doubt – to marvel at the facilities Herod had built in it. He ensured storage of water, food, weapons and creature comforts. In such a fortress Herod and his entourage felt safe. Because he liked it, he built one alongside it – one as a palace, and the other as his office. In 73 AD 960 Jews took refuge in this fortress, when the Romans attacked. Sadly, they could not hold out for long and committed suicide, rather than surrender to the Romans. The castle is now a World Heritage Site.

Even at 76, Herod was obsessed with ill-gotten power and loathed a usurper. That is why he ordered the slaughter of infants, when the three wise men did not return to inform him of the whereabouts of Baby Jesus – who he feared would usurp his throne. He hoped that the slaughter of children would cancel his embarrassment. He ruled with an iron hand and added to the splendour of his palaces, one of which was the Herodium – almost a fortress. Now and again he tried to appease the locals, but they did not trust him. When he died, his sons took over.

When Herod Archelaus, son of Herod the Great, failed to keep order in his part of the Kingdom, Emperor Augustus removed him from office. That province – Judea – was given to governor Pontius Pilate to administer. Herod Antipas and Herod Philip, like Archelaus, were given other parts of the land to manage. They too owed loyalty to Rome who gave them coveted positions. Jesus was sent to Herod Antipas by Pilate, since Herod oversaw the territory Jesus came from. Antipas poked fun at Jesus, but was wary of getting involved, since he smelled a plot.

Sea of Galilee: It is a lake, not a sea, fed by the Jordan River. It is about 21 kilometers long and 12 kilometers wide. It is about 642 feet below sea level and 150 feet deep in some parts, and prone to unexpected squalls – with wind from the surrounding hills whipping up mountain-like waves. We recall that the disciples of Jesus, seasoned fishermen, were terrified of the storm, which Jesus calmed. He did the same thing on another occasion. When he rebuked the storm, it subsided.

On some occasions, Jesus sat in a boat and taught the crowds, who packed the shore. A boat – 27 feet long and 7.5 feet wide, which could accommodate 13 people – similar to the one Jesus and his disciples used, was discovered by archaeologists in 1986. The boat is housed in the Yigai Allon Museum, at Ginossar.

The Sea of Galilee – the largest source of drinking water of that region - was known by other names: Lake of Gennesaret, Sea of Tiberias, Lake of Tiberias, Sea of Chinnereth. At that time there were 10 towns on the shores of the sea. Of them, Gennesaret, Tiberias, and Chinnereth were among the more popular.

On the shores of this sea, Jesus invited Peter and Andrew, and John and James, to be his disciples. On the same shore, Jesus hosted breakfast for his weary and disillusioned disciples – after his resurrection.

Kidron Valley: It was a place of olive groves, and a deep ravine channeling a stream. It was the route David took, when fleeing from his son Absalom. The Pillar of Absalom in the valley, is 22 meters tall. Jesus often walked the valley, on his way to and from places he visited. The valley is known to hold the tombs of Jehoshaphat, the fourth king of Judah, and Zechariah, father of John the Baptist. But history is rubbished today, as sewage flows through the valley.

Armageddon: Armageddon, otherwise known as Megiddo, in the Jezreel Valley, brings on a shiver as we read Rev. 16: 16. It will be the place of our final judgement on the last day. The place where the good and bad will be separated – the good finding a place in heaven and the bad cast into hell. King Solomon built a city and fortress in the valley, that witnessed many battles and the flow of much blood.

Bethsaida: In this town, now located in the Muslim Quarter of Jerusalem, Jesus was active as a preacher and healer. Mk. 8: 22-26 reports on a miracle Jesus performed on a blind man of this town. From this shore Jesus walked the waters on the Sea of Galilee, and not far from this place he fed 5000. Some scholars speculate that there were two towns by the same name, though there is not much evidence to support their claims. A little after Jesus died, Philip, son of Herod the Great, renamed the town – Bethsaida Julias (in honor of the Emperor's wife) - after raising the town to the level of a city. Peter, his brother Andrew, and Philip came from this town.

Caesarea Philippi: The city was built by Philip, son of Herod the great, who cleverly added his name to that of Caesar, the Roman Emperor. The city is located at the source of the Jordan river, and is therefore fertile. The river connects the Sea of Galilee with the Dead Sea. The city served as the administrative capital of the Romans and was a major port on the Mediterranean Sea. In this river John the Baptist baptized Jesus, when the Holy Spirit descended on Him and God the Father spoke of his beloved Son (Mt. 2: 13-17). Mt. 16: 18-19 records the event of Jesus giving Peter the keys to the kingdom of heaven, at this place.

The Wailing Wall

"Jerusalem --- For I tell you, you will not see me again until you say, 'Blessed is the one who comes in the name of the Lord.'" Mt. 23: 39

Sea of Galilee

"As he walked the Sea of Galilee, he saw two brothers, Simon, who is called Peter, and Andrew his brother, casting a net into the sea – for they were fishermen. And he said to them, "Follow me, and I will make you fish for people." Mt. 4: 18-19.

Tiberias: It was a fashionable town built by Herod Antipas, on the west shore of the Sea of Galilee, to honor Tiberius Caesar, the Emperor. He made it the capital city in 18 BC, but people were reluctant to settle in the town, because it was built over a cemetery – considered unclean by the Jews. With 17 natural hot springs, it was a popular destination for recreation and healing. Jesus avoided such fashionable towns. Instead, he chose to work in the fishing community and among the destitute – offering them healing and teaching.

Caesarea: In Israel, it was the administrative capital of Rome, that Herod the Great built. The town is recalled a few times in Scripture. Acts 10: 44-48 reports the baptizing of the early Christians. Acts 9: 30 records Paul's journey to Tarsus, through Caesarea. Acts 18: 21-22 states that Paul leaves Ephesus to land at Caesarea. And, in Acts 25: 4, Festus was to meet Paul at Caesarea.

Jaffa (Joppa): It is believed to have been founded by Japheth, son of Noah – one of the oldest towns in Israel. Jonah embarked for Tarshih from here. Peter was here in the house of Simon, the tanner, where he had the vision of pure and impure animals, to give him the message that even the Gentiles were welcome into the Christian fold. The Armenian convent in Jaffa, served as a hospital for the troops of Napoleon, during his expedition to the Holy Land.

Samaria: King Omri made Samaria the capital of Israel , the northern kingdom of the ten tribes. Jerusalem was the capital of Judah, the kingdom of the two remaining tribes. Micah, prophesied the destruction of Samaria, which happened as the Assyrians overran the place, when the kings of Israel repeatedly *"did evil in the sight of God"*.

Jesus visited the place and met the local people after he encountered the woman at the well. Such initiatives were frowned upon by the Jewish Elders, because Samaritans were not considered to be pure Jews. Tactfully, Jesus brought into his parable the role of a Samaritan who saved the life of a traveller – beaten by bandits. In place of an inn on the highway between Jerusalem and Jericho - the place where the Samaritan lodged the wounded man – now stands a museum. In citing the Samaritan, not a Jew, Jesus swept away cobwebs that had accumulated over years of disregard for the community. He meant: If God is our Father, then all are our brothers and sisters.

Why were the Samaritans despised? Assyria, a powerful nation at that time, conquered the region in 722 BC (2 Kings 17) and took Jews as captives to Assyria. To make up for the numbers, they settled Assyrians in the area. In time the descendants of the Assyrian-Jewish couples came to be known as Samaritans – despised by Jews who considered them impure.

Besides visits by Jesus, his disciples Peter, John and Philip visited the place, after Jesus ascended to heaven. In the early Christians, the disciples of Jesus found diamonds in a coal-pit.

Qumran: The place is about 15 kilometers south of Jericho. In 1947 a Bedouin shepherd, Mohammed Ahmed el-Hamed, found seven clay jars in which he found scrolls wrapped in linen, that had been preserved for about 2000 years. It is estimated that there were about 850 scrolls, covering events in the Old Testament. The longest among them was 8 meters long. They were written in Hebrew, Aramaic and Greek, on parchment and papyrus. There was no mention of Jesus, in the scrolls. They were supposedly written by Essenes, a tribe following an austere lifestyle – Joseph, Mary's husband was from this tribe. This group is also known as the Dead Sea Sect. Of the scrolls found, seven are housed in the Shrine of the Book, part of the Israel Museum. Six of them are written in Hebrew, and one in Aramaic.

Dobrath: It is also known as Daburiya. Some refer to it as Zebulum, named after the tenth son of Jacob. Now it an Arabic village at the foot of Mount Tabor. Lk. 9: 37-43 reports on the miracle that Jesus performed, in this place, on an epileptic boy. The disciples of Jesus could not rid the boy of the demon, that had possessed and tormented him. It needed the power of the Son of Man to bring healing to the boy and solace to his father.

Field of blood: It got its name from the dastardly act of Judas – who betrayed his Master. When he felt a tinge of remorse over his horrendous deed, he returned 30 pieces of silver to the priests who had given him the bribe. They refused to accept the money, since it was blood money. Instead, they bought a plot to be used for burying strangers. The plot which was near the Hinnon Valley, was rich in clay. Therefore, potters extracted clay from it for their work.

Mount of Olives: Mount Olivet is one of the three hills on the long ridge to the east of Jerusalem. It is the location of many Biblical events. From its peak – 800 meters high – one gets a good view of the Old City. During David's time it was covered with Olive trees, giving it its name. King David fled through it and the Kidron Valley to escape his son (2 Sam.15: 30). Later, on the same site King Solomon built pagan temples to appease his foreign wives. On that hill Ezekiel had a vision of the glory of God. The hill figures in Zachariah's prophesy that the Lord of Hosts would stand on the Mount of Olives. Jesus frequented the mount, and prayed there before his arrest. Now it is the site of many churches – Churches of all Nations, Saint Mary Magdalene, Dominus Flevit, Pater Noster, Dome of Ascension, and Grotto of Gethsemane. Much earlier it was a Jewish cemetery for over 3000 years, with over 1,50,000 graves in it.

Mount Zion: It is also known as Mount Sion, a symbol of the Promised Land. It was the highest point in ancient Jerusalem, and is near the Armenian Quarter. Important events took place on Mount Zion. 1) David was buried there. Muslims also respect David, so his tomb was not destroyed even during the Muslim invasion. In the Old

Testament Jerusalem was known as the city of David, after he captured it from the Jebusites. Then he built his capital there. 2) Solomon built the temple on Mount Zion. 3) Then it became the site for the mother of all churches – Hagia Sion, which was later destroyed. 4) Historic events took place in the Upper Room. 5) Jesus was investigated by the high priests, after his capture. 6) The tomb of Mary is located there. 7) The Council of Jerusalem in 50 AD was held there – where the status of Gentile Christians was discussed. 8) Oskar Schindler, hero of 1098 Jews whom he rescued from the Nazis, was buried there. His life was made famous by Steven Spielberg, through his movie Schindler's List.

Pool of Bethzatha: It was also known as the Sheep Gate. John 5: 1 – 18 reports on a miracle at the pool. It was a pool were people swam – not like the pools we have today. An angel visited the pool and stirred the water. Those who quickly stepped into the water, after the angel had stirred it, were healed. A paralytic who sat on the steps of the pool for 38 years, and could not enter the water, remained afflicted. Jesus, hearing of his plight, healed him to the amazement of onlookers.

What strikes one is Jesus' courtesy. He asks the man: *"Do you want to be made well?"* No compulsion, no brash behaviour of an insolent benefactor – only cordiality and good manners even when doing the man a favour. Jesus does not introduce himself or give him a list of miracles to convince him. That would be in bad taste, he knows. So, subtly he performs the miracle. How much like Jesus are we? We like to trumpet our achievements, publish our credentials and call attention to ourselves. What a contrast!

Many doubted that such a place existed, until archaeologists discovered clear traces of it, beneath the ruins of an old church.

Pool of Siloam: John 9: 1- 41 has a long narration of the miracle that takes place at the pool. Jesus heals a blind man, who he instructs to wash the mud off his eyes, in the pool. A church, named after Our Savior the Illuminator was built on that spot. In 614 the church was destroyed, and not rebuilt. The property, rediscovered in 2004, after centuries of neglect, now belongs to the Greek Orthodox Church. In Nehemiah 3:15, the place is referred to as King's Garden.

Emmaus: The place is 7 miles from Jerusalem. In 1902 a church was built on that site, although builders were uncertain of where the house of Cleopas stood. That does not matter, as long as every Christian recalls that Jesus walked with him and his friend, for some distance, before breaking bread with the two. Jesus was incognito, but they felt the warmth of his presence – even as we shall on the tour.

CHAPTER THREE

The Old Testament - Harking Back to Moses

"For my thoughts are not your thoughts, nor are your ways, my ways" Isaiah 55: 8.

Pillar of Salt: The best place to begin is the beginning – Genesis. God's wrath was stirred by the sins of Sodom and Gomorrah, and he decided to bring them to a fiery end, despite Abraham pleading with him to spare them. When Abraham could not produce even ten people who were faithful to God, in the cursed land, he had to accept God's judgement. Before God let that happen, he instructed Lot and his family to flee the destruction, with a caution: They were not to turn around and look at the havoc. They fled, but Lot's wife could not resist the temptation of looking back. Instantly she became a Pillar of Salt.

Driving down Jericho Road (which is northeast of Jerusalem, west of Jordan River, about six miles north of the Dead Sea, and reputed to be the oldest city, with a history going back to 8500 BC), we do not miss the pillar of salt, which was once Lot's wife. Though age has withered the pillar, the form of a woman in flight can be discerned. Here is an instance of disobedience, and its consequences (Gen. 19: 26).

The black topped road that we traveled from Jericho looked like a huge black serpent slithering between dense mountains. Jesus referred to this road in his parable, the Good Samaritan (Lk. 10: 25-37). He spoke of bandits lurking behind cover, ready to pounce on unsuspecting travelers. The mountains, across many miles, provide cover for those with nefarious intent. The picture that Jesus painted comes to mind vividly, as we look at the unending black mass of rock.

Reflection: Do we stop to ponder why God does not punish us instantly when we wilfully disobey him? It is because his mercy exceeds his justice. In justice he had to act with Sodom and Gomorrah, because they had spurned his warnings and mercy many times. Let us be warned against taking his mercy for granted, lest he invoke his justice!

Under what rocks are we concealing our black agenda? Under the guise of goodness are we hiding our devious plots to malign and discredit our neighbors? Is ours a mask of holiness waiting to be torn apart?

Burning Bush: In different parts of the Holy Land the story of Moses is told. Imagine watching a bush burn, without the flames consuming the bush! That was Moses' experience. Curious to know more, he goes close to the bush, only to hear the voice of God, who commissions him to go to Egypt. As slaves, the Jews had suffered for many years in Egypt. God heard their prayers and was to send them a deliverer, in the person of Moses. Why did God choose Moses to lead the Jews out of Egypt? He was a murderer, an absconder and one who stammered. Yet, God chose him, because his thoughts are not ours. He uses the weak to accomplish great deeds. *"If God only used perfect people. Nothing would ever get done." Rick Warren*

Reflection: Standing before the Burning Bush we are in awe of Moses, who heard the voice of God. Perhaps God is planning to use us in wondrous ways, if only we lend an ear to his voice. Are we ready to accept his mission – big or small? Have we found our purpose in life? Are we willing to fulfil it?

Parting of the sea: We are familiar with the Exodus – the escape of the Jews from Egypt, led by Moses. There is a spot, though no one is sure, of the Parting of the Sea, where the Jews crossed the sea dry-shod. At that spot we recall the faith of Moses. Before him was the turbulent sea and behind him were howling Jews, cursing and swearing. Where was he to lead his people, when there was no way out? He trusted in God and commanded the sea, which obeyed. It is an inspiration to read chapters 14 and 15 of Exodus, to get a feel of the event and to assess the character of Moses, as he praises God. One word, which I seldom use comes to mind – AWESOME – as I picture Moses, staff in hand, order the sea, and the sea parting to permit the terrified Jews to cross. The Ten Commandments, my favorite movie, captures the scene splendidly.

Reflection: When we are confronted with obstacles and hurdles that we find difficult to cross, do we surrender to the will of God and beg him to carry us over the blocks? Is our faith strong enough? Will those behind us be edified by our staunch faith?

Marah: After crossing the sea, Moses had more problems to solve. At Marah (bitter) the Jews thirst, but there is only bitter water. The teeming millions begin to taunt him. Imagine life in the desert without water! Moses is helpless, so he turns to God.

Church near the site of the burning bush

" I am who I am" Ex. 3: 14.

God instructs him to throw a piece of wood into the water. Bitter water turns sweet, and the Jews quench their thirst. God could have changed bitter water into sweet water without the piece of wood or without Moses, yet he uses both. Why? Because God glories in partnerships. He wants his creatures to be involved and he chooses the manner in which such partnerships will be sealed.

Reflection: Is there some bitterness in our lives? Some relationship that is souring? Some task neglected? Some help not given or accepted? Even if we hate to admit it, such lapses, in an ugly heap, make our life bitter. It is time we turned to God to beg for his intervention. He does not refuse. He will come with hands filled with gifts, when we humbly surrender to his holy will.

Elim: We drive on and pass Elim. It had twelve springs and seventy palm trees when Moses and the Jews halted there (Ex. 15:27). A few palm trees still grow in the region, but not many springs quench the thirst of the ground and that of passers-by. Soon after Elim, we pass Rephidim, where Moses struck the rock and let water spout from it (Ex. 17: 1-7). At Rephidim the Jews had to fight Amalek. While Joshua engaged them in battle, Moses held up his staff. As long as his staff was raised, the Jews won. When his hands sagged, the Jews lost. So, they propped up his hands with stones, until sundown, when Joshua and his men beat Amalek (Ex. 17: 8-13).

Reflection: We notice that God continually works miracles for Moses and the Jews, despite the callous behaviour of the majority. Why? Because Moses, his chosen, was strong in his faith and repeatedly interceded with God for his mercy. Do we trust God, like Moses did? Do we raise our hands in supplication and praise?

Mount Sinai: It is a key stop on the tour. We recall God giving Moses the Ten Commandments on the mountain (Ex. 20). As he descends the mountains, after forty days, with the tablets of stone, on which the Ten Commandments were seared, he finds the Jews shaping a golden calf (Ex. 32), and Aaron, his brother conniving with the Jews in the act. When Moses sees the desecration, he flings the tablets to the ground, causing death and destruction. And, God sends a plague on the troublemakers.

Reflection: The same commandments that God gave the Jews he gives to us. Yet, we break them with impunity. Should we not thank God for sparing us from destruction, the way he did the Jews? Shall we resolve to keep sacred the commandments of God – restraining ourselves from sins of lust, refraining from sins of killing others, by character assassination - desisting from sins of theft of even a trifle, and loving God above everything else in our lives?

Bronze Snake: As the Jews move on, they reach a point where snakes sting them, some fatally. Moses is in distress. How can he protect his people? As always, he turns to God. Build a bronze snake, God commands; and lift it up for the Jews to look at. They will be healed, he promises (Num. 21: 9). At about the same spot, a replica of the bronze snake stands tall. The symbol was a forerunner of what would happen centuries later when Jesus would be raised on a cross for humankind to look at and gain salvation. The good thief was the first to find his way to Paradise, by looking at Jesus on the cross.

Reflection: What does the crucifix mean to us? Do we see salvation in it? Is it our strength and refuge? Are we proud of our crucified Savior? Do we proclaim him to those who do not know him?

Promised Land: In stages the Jews progress on their journey to the Promised Land. But there is a startling development: Moses will not cross over with them. Since he did not diligently follow God's instructions when striking the rock for water, when the Jews were thirsty, God forbids him from entering the promised land. As a consolation prize, God allows Moses to see the promised land from the vantage point of Mount Nebo (Deut. 34: 1). He sees the Promised Land and is filled with wonder and gratitude. He dies on Mount Nebo and is buried in the valley of the land of Moab, opposite Bethpeor (Deut. 34: 6). But no one knows the exact spot, although a memorial slab approximates the site. A beautiful church crowns the hilltop, and a small museum displays ancient exhibits.

Standing on Mount Nebo, with a gentle breeze wafting from the valley, we find the view breath-taking. God's munificence in giving them the land of milk and honey is unmatched. He is true to his promises. Taking in the view, it seemed to me that God dropped a large blanket of earth to the ground. As it descended, it formed ups and downs, hills and valleys, in undulating splendour. The pity is that God's gift became the battleground of warring groups; now it lies wasted. It is not what it was then. We spot patches of green in barren brown, dotted with small bodies of water, like oases of hope. On a clear day, with a powerful binoculars, Jerusalem and Bethlehem are visible in the distance. Reverence for those places begins there – on Mount Nebo - and culminates when we set foot on sacred soil. As we drive on the road that skirts hills and valleys, we are reminded of a large community of Jews who walked the land in search of a home, and peace.

Reflection: Do we recognize God's gifts to us - Life itself, family and loved ones, talents and work, leisure and friends, freedom and the gift of choice, and the promise of salvation? Do we use our gifts to serve God and our neighbour? He gave the Jews a land of milk and honey; he has given us more, if only we add up our gifts.

Treated unfairly: Moses, the prophet who met God face to face, was denied the crown. He carried the cross without dissent and was faithful to God over long years of leading a defiant people. But all his obedience was struck down with one act of disobedience. We tend to empathize with Moses, as we see God treating him rather unfairly. Since God is infinitely just and merciful, we cannot wallow in pity for Moses. We have to look for a reason that made God deprive Moses of the reward of entering the promised land. We have a clue in what Jesus said many years later:

Where more is given, more is expected. Moses was unusually blessed. Every request of his was granted, every prayer answered. From his tangled past God elevated him to be the leader of the Jews. So, God expected of him absolute obedience – nothing short of it. When he failed to carry out God's instruction, he unwittingly paid a huge price. But watch God compensate him, because he is never outdone in generosity. At the Transfiguration of Jesus, Moses is made a partner. Imagine the height to which God exalted him at that moment! What better reward could Moses expect? Unlike most of us who feel cheated when we suspect that we are treated unfairly, Moses did not protest. He did not incite the Jews to rebel against God. He accepted God's verdict, because he knew that God is never wrong.

Reflection: What is our response when we imagine that we are treated unfairly? Nothing can make us worthy of the gifts of life, only less unworthy. We sulk, blame others and God, and wait for a chance to hit back. Is it a mature response? Let us learn from Moses to be humble and accept the vicissitudes of life with prudence and faith – with love of God, above all. He is fairest of all! *"Where love is, there is God also." Leo Tolstoy*

The Old Testament – King David and Prophet Elijah

"God does not demand that I be successful. God demands that I be faithful." Mother Teresa

King David: After reliving history with Moses and learning from him, we invite another stalwart – David – to share some lessons with us. As a shepherd boy he challenges the giant Goliath, not because of his strength or brilliance, but trust in God. Soon he gains the attention of King Saul, for whom he plays the harp (1. Sam. 16: 23). A bronze painted image of David playing the harp is a popular tourist attraction. Samuel, the prophet, anoints him as king, though David has many older brothers. Through prudent administration and daring skills in battle, he consolidates his kingdom.

But the life of David was not all roses. Thorns hurt him from time to time. Before he took the throne, he had to face the envy of King Saul, who set traps for him and hunted him relentlessly. Although David had a chance to slay King Saul, he would not because he was the anointed one. God's blessings were with David and he was saved from death at the hands of King Saul. After he became King, his son tried to kill him and usurp the throne. He had to flee, yet again. What hurt him grievously was the treachery of his own flesh. Despite these travails, David was faithful to God and sang his praises, even in his darkest hour. In the Book of Psalms, his contribution is massive – of the 150 psalms, 73 are composed by him and he is credited with two more, because of their style. It meant that 50% of all the psalms were composed by David.

Despite his wisdom and goodness, God forbids him from constructing the Temple – a holy task he had yearned to perform. But God explains: His hands are soiled with blood through many battles. The Temple needed cleaner hands. His son Solomon is delegated with the task of Temple-building. God's justice which appears to be under cloud when David's request is denied, moves out of the cloud to bless Solomon lavishly – to become the wisest man the world will ever know. He is also blessed with riches beyond his wildest dreams and a reign of peace. Why does Solomon receive these gifts? Because he chose wisdom over riches, not long life or fame, when God asked him what he wanted. God blesses David through his son Solomon. As we know, no one outdoes God in generosity.

Was David envious of his son? Did he rebel against God? Did he instigate the Jews to turn against God? Did his love of God diminish? Instead, we find that he grows in love and thanksgiving, praising God even in his despair. Truly a man after God's own heart!

Another thorn that hurt him was his infidelity. His lust drove him to adultery with Bathsheba, his neighbor's wife, and murder of her husband. But when prophet Nathan comes to him and narrates a story, he repents, and makes amends. In time, David dies and is buried. A tomb marks the spot where he was laid to rest, though some dispute the location.

Reflection: Like us, David sinned. But what made him stand out among grave sinners was his deep contrition and penance. His psalms are a testimony of his cry to God for forgiveness. Like David, do we repent when we offend God? Does our sorrow find expression in our resolve not to sin again?

Treated unfairly: David was denied the privilege of building the Temple, but he did not complain or hold it against God. Instead of fighting God through an attitude of entitlement, like David do we accept God's will, which is always the best, because no one has the infinite wisdom of God, and no one loves us like God does.

Like David, ancestor of Jesus, do we use the talents God has given us. He was given a talent in music, which he developed to glorify God. What talent in us is idling?

Prophet Elijah: Centuries pass since David died. Now King Ahab and his wife Jezebel rule over Israel. It is a testing time for Elijah, the prophet of God. The false prophets – 450 of them – draw people away from God. In sheer frustration, Elijah demands of the Jews a choice: *"If the Lord is God follow him; but if Baal, then follow him"* (1 Kings 18: 21). In a cave, now marked by a church on Mount Carmel, Elijah, the faithful prophet, prays for God's help. Then he challenges the false prophets to a test. Let us see whose prayers are answered? The false prophets go first. They offer prayers to Baal, imploring him to consume their sacrifice. Nothing happens.

Then it is the turn of Elijah. He prays to God to devour his sacrifice. In moments a fire descends from heaven to consume his sacrifice, to the consternation of the royal couple and the assembled Baal devotees. The people then move over to the side of Elijah and glorify God. Mount Carmel (Muhraka) in northern Israel is near the modern hi-tech city of Haifa, where Stella Maris, a church built in honor of Mary, celebrates the triumph of Elijah.

"David took the lyre and played it with his hand." 1 Sam. 16:23

A bronze painted statue of David with his lyre is a popular attraction

Reflection: Like the Jews of old, do we vacillate between God and other options? Are our attachments to wealth, possessions, fame and relationship stronger than our bond with God? Do we trust astrologers, collect charms to ward off evil, and surround ourselves with powders and lotions and trinkets to protect us from harm? Do we skip Sunday Service to attend talks by Gurus and chants by frenzied followers of such con men? Isn't it time that we returned to the true God, like the people of Elijah's time?

The face of God: In the Old Testament we are puzzled at the way God acts – sometimes mercifully, at other times sternly – punishing even small offenses (disobedience of Lot's wife, Moses' disobedience and similar acts of negligence).

Scripture is best understood when we comprehend the spirit, the essence, and not the words, literally. For example: Pluck out your eye and cut out your limb would mean that most of us would be blind and without limbs, at the rate at which we sin. The Compassionate Jesus did not mean to deprive us of his gifts. Instead, he planned to caution us: As much as you value your eyes and limbs, value your imperishable soul and avoid the occasions of sin.

In the Old Testament, God sometimes showed a stern face because he was dealing with a rebellious people who believed in entitlement, just because they were children of Abraham. So, to teach them, God alternates mercy and justice to alternate with their moods of prayer and stubborn refusal to comply. He was teaching them, using different methods.

The stern face of God in the Old Testament gives way to the compassionate face of Jesus (Second Person of the Blessed Trinity – God Himself) in the New Testament, with his infinite mercy exceeding his justice. So, we see more of forgiveness – a virtue that he taught and lived. Now, his teaching takes on a new form.

The words of Isaiah are a revelation: *"For my thoughts are not your thoughts, nor are your ways, my ways"* Isaiah 55:8. His thoughts and ways are inscrutable. So, trying to fathom the true meaning of his words can be a perilous task, with our limited intelligence – when his wisdom is infinite.

Jesus' words: *"The Father and I are one"* only confirm the union in the Holy Trinity. Although we attribute creation to the Father, redemption to the Son and sanctification to the Holy Spirit, they are one and inseparable. They act in love, in our best interest and for our salvation. *"Whoever does not love does not know God, for God is love." 1 Jn. 4: 8.* So, let us expect from God only mercy and love.

Reflection: It is time we internalized this truth. Rejoice! God is LOVE – full of infinite mercy. His mercy is not limited by our response to him. Since he is love, he can act only in love. Isn't it fair that we respond in love, out of sheer decency? If we are chastised, it is because of his love – not wanting us to suffer from eternal pain and suffering. So, the next time we suffer, let us look beyond the apparent to find the merciful hand of our Savior. *"God whispers to us in our joys, speaks to us in our difficulties, and shouts to us in our pain." C S Lewis*

CHAPTER FIVE

The New Testament – the early part of Jesus' life

"The love of God is the only love that is higher than a mother's love; all others are lower." Swami Vivekananda

Although I try to follow the sequence in Matthew's Gospel, the order may change now and again, because other Gospel writers shuffle the sequence.

Mary's Parents: No son loved his mother more than Jesus loved Mary. And, no mother loved her son as much as Mary loved Jesus. Their love was so pure and celestial that we can only marvel at it, and pray that a spark from it ignites our love for the two. Therefore, it is fitting that we start the early part of Jesus' life, with Mary. She was the daughter of Saints Joachim and Anne (like them, both saints, the parents of the Little Flower are also saints. Great parents of great daughters!) As pious parents who upheld the Law, they instructed Mary even in her childhood. So raised, she spent part of her life in God's House, away from her parents. **Saint Anne's Church** marks the place where Mary was born. God chose her to be his mother, and to fight the serpent (Gen. 3: 15).

After her engagement to Joseph, who was a widower, Mary is taken by surprise when an angel visits her to announce her key role in salvation, as the mother of Jesus (Lk. 1: 26-38). In the **Basilica of the Annunciation**, in Nazareth, a grotto celebrates what was once Mary's home. The church has a dome that is 55-meters high – to symbolize her tall stature in the eyes of God.

Reflection: What is our attitude to our parents? Does it resemble that of Mary? As an obedient child she lived the standards set by her parents – obedience to God's will. She demonstrated the teaching of her parents with great conviction, when she surrendered her will to the will of God, in accepting to be his mother. She did not know what was in store for her but she said yes, because she trusted in the goodness of God and his unconditional love. Do we accept the will of God, even when we do not understand its meaning and purpose?

Ein Karem: It is about six kilometres away from the Old City of Jerusalem – a place reserved for Levites, the priestly tribe of that time. There we visit the home of John the Baptist, whose parents are Zachariah and Elizabeth. Although we know the story, it is worth recalling. Elizabeth, Mary's cousin and Zachariah are childless, and old. They have given up hope of having a child. That is why Zachariah protests when the angel announces to him that he will have a son, to be named John. Responding to his rebuke, the angel makes him speechless. Only after the birth of John, is his tongue loosed. When it happens he praises God for the gift of a son. A picture of his prayer, which appears on the compound walls of the church, follows. John, the last in the line of prophets, is the forerunner of the Savior.

It is also the place where Mary sings the Magnificat – in praise of God's goodness and her nothingness. The cousins meet in ecstasy and John leaps in the womb of his mother. At that instant the Holy Spirit cleanses him of original sin. Mary was born sinless. John was freed of sin, even before he was born. The translation of the Magnificat, in different languages, appears on the compound walls of a church. A photograph of the prayer, for your edification, is captured on one of the following pages. Not far from John's house is Mary's Spring – where Mary collects water, when she is visiting her cousin.

Two churches are built in close proximity. One, the **Church of Saint John the Baptist**, is managed by Catholics, and the other by the Eastern Orthodox Church.

Reflection: Mary is with child. Yet she travels a long distance to visit her cousin to help her. In her circumstances, what would we do? Wallow in self-pity, because we have problems and shorten our hands to help. Or, would we change our night to day for the sake of others?

In the Magnificat, Mary praises God for blessings that are beyond her hopes. She is not puffed up with her new importance. Instead, she gives all credit to God. How do we respond, when we are blessed? Do we connect the blessing to our worth? To our talents and hard work? To our entitlement? Can we learn from Mary to give all credit and glory to God?

Christmas: The greatest event in Mary's life happens next. Jesus, the Son of God is born to her (Lk. 2: 1-7). The **Church of the Nativity**, in which a shining star marks the spot where Jesus was born, celebrates God becoming man. Entry to the church is through a door only 1.5 meters high, where visitors have to crouch to enter, reminding them of the humility of Jesus. God humbled himself to become man. A grotto is built around the star.

Reflection: The birth of God as man is difficult for humans to comprehend. Imagine a king born in a hut! Not likely. Now imagine the King of Kings born in a cave! We are amazed at the extent to which Jesus goes to teach us humility. When he said: Learn of me, for I am meek and humble of heart, he was setting us an unequalled example. Unlike him, what do we do? We strut on the stage of life to brag and boast of our distinguished family, our riches, our possessions, our connections, and our achievements. We place store by perishables, when our imperishable soul is starved of essentials – a contrite and humble disposition. And what of Jesus' love or us? Leaving his heavenly home, he resides in our midst. Would we give up our status in life to live among the destitute and oppressed?

The Shepherd's Field: Jesus continues his lessons for us. He does not announce his birth to King Herod or the Elders of the Sanhedrin, but to poor and humble shepherds, who were watching over their sheep at night (Lk. 2: 8-18). The Shepherd's Field is about three kilometres from Bethlehem. Three churches are built on that field:

1) Church of the Shepherds is built and maintained by the Greek Orthodox Church.

2) Church of Angels is managed by the Catholic Church.

3) The Protestant Shepherd Field is run by the protestants. The three churches honor the shepherds and angels – the two parties to the Christmas announcement.

Reflection: People were used to seeing kings in their grandeur, but the shepherd see something different. Their simplicity exalts them to the wisdom of seeing God in an infant, and in a cave. They worship him. Jesus is in the unlikeliest places – not among the rich and famous, but among the poor, the suffering, the destitute. Do we recognize him in those around us? Is our behaviour to others motivated by the belief that Jesus is in them – as Mother Teresa discovered?

The three Wise Men: From a distance, in the East, three wise men travel, freighted with gifts, to meet and worship the newborn king. They are led by a star in the high heavens, across the desert sands, only to arrive at Herod's palace to seek direction to the abode of the new king. Herod feigns respect for the new king and promises to visit him, if the three men would return to give him the route.When they do not return, he feels cheated and unleashes a reign of terror, killing all infants below the age of two. The heart-rending cries of mothers fills the air, but Herod is not deterred. He will chase the little king until he kills him, he swears.

Zachariah's Prayer

Enter Caption

"And you, child will be called the prophet of the Most High;"

Lk. 1: 76

Reflection: The feast of the Epiphany celebrates the manifestation of Jesus to the world. It is fitting that kings and wise men come to worship the King of Kings. They bring Jesus gold to signify his kingship, frankincense to celebrate his priesthood and Godhead, and myrrh to commemorate his role as a victim for our sins. They would carry the message to the far corners of the world. The epiphany continues when the angels announce the birth of Jesus to the shepherds. It repeats at the Baptism of Jesus, when the Holy Spirit descends on him and God the Father speaks. It happens again at the Transfiguration of Jesus, when Moses and Elijah visit him and God the Father speaks. We are assigned the task of manifesting Jesus in our lives. How do we do it?

Egypt: Joseph is instructed, in a dream, to flee to Egypt. The Holy Family travels over many hundred kilometres to reach Egypt – Mary with Baby Jesus on a donkey and Joseph walking alongside. They cannot anchor in one place, because the soldiers of Herod pursue them. So, they shift their dwelling many times. A map outside the church – built to commemorate their first stop in Egypt – traces the course of their shifts. After the death of Herod, the Holy Family returns to Nazareth and lives there until Jesus is thirty years old and ready for his ministry.

Reflection: The three Wise Men travel a long distance to worship Jesus. They bring with them gifts. How often do we visit our churches to meet Jesus and pay him homage, with gifts of our sincere and contrite hearts?

Think of Herod, a proxy king, chasing the King of kings. We might not aim for the throne, but we want to live our lives the way we fancy, chasing Jesus away from our hearts when we choose honor, power, wealth and pleasure, as deities we worship. The pain he suffered as an infant, he relives, each time we choose somebody or something over him.

Think of Joseph, who does not question God's plan. He will obey at once – despite the difficulties he will face. He does not argue: Why does not God do away with Herod, the evil one? Instead, God dispatches his own son, at the dead of night, on a perilous journey to a distant land. Although it did not make sense to Joseph, he does not delay his departure with Mary and Jesus, but trusts that God would do what

The Magnificat

"Surely, from now on all generations will call me blessed; for the Mighty One has done great things for me," Lk. 1: 48-49.

is best for them. How do we reason? Do we try to make sense of all that happens to us, instead of trusting in Providence?

Home of the Holy Family: In Nazareth, which 1300 feet above sea level, we visit the home of the Holy Family and Joseph's workshop. In Saint Joseph's Church, a crypt marks the site where the home once stood. After their stay in Egypt, the Holy Family settles in Nazareth, and Joseph gets busy providing for the family through his carpentry skills. Tradition has it that a huge building was being constructed in the vicinity of their home, where Joseph found work and Jesus worked as his apprentice.

Reflection: In Mt.1: 19 Joseph is called a righteous man – morally upright. Why? The Gospels do not provide much information on Joseph, but the little there is speaks of his sterling character. He does not want to disgrace Mary, when he learns that she is with child. He plans to break the engagement to her, without the danger of her being stoned for adultery. Later, when the angel allays his fears, he readily takes Mary as his wife, and becomes the dependable foster-father of Jesus. Each time he receives a message from God he obeys immediately, and does not argue or rebel, as the Jews of that time did. Truly he was a man of God – righteous!

Will people who know us call us righteous? Why not? What is disfiguring our character? In what way are we not morally upright?

Baptism of Jesus: As Jesus is busy in the workshop that Joseph built, John the Baptist, his cousin, is preaching on repentance. People flock to hear the man who eats locusts and drinks wild honey, and is clothed in camel's hair (Mk.1:6). Soon, Jesus joins the crowds and asks John to baptise him, in the Jordan River. John is taken aback, but obeys Jesus. We know what follows – God the Father speaks, and God the Holy Spirit descends on Jesus in the form of a dove. At the Jordan River which connects the Rea Sea with the Dead Sea, we watch people go through another baptism.

Reflection: In Mt. 11:11, we read of the praise Jesus showers on John the Baptist – no ordinary man, but one who was fearless and mission-driven. What kind of example are we setting for those around us – in the family, in the workplace, in the neighbourhood? Are we shedding light or casting shadows? Like John the Baptist, are we defending our convictions – not accepting or giving bribes, not speaking ill of others, not doing harm to others in any way? With his life, John paid the price of defending his beliefs. Do we make compromises when challenged by ultimatums?

Jesus does not have to receive baptism – he is sinless. Yet, he sets us an example: 1) To affirm John in his mission. 2) To give a lead to others in the land. 3) To start his ministry on the right note. With the Father and Holy Spirit manifesting themselves, we find the Holy Trinity in action. When we follow Jesus and his baptism through our baptism, we are gaining entry into the mystical body of Christ – his Church. What are we doing that will edify others? Does our baptism mean anything to us, other than a ritual we were made to perform as children? In what way are we different from those who have not been baptised? When we renew our baptism vows, do we reflect on what they mean?

Fast in the desert: Before Jesus starts his ministry he decides to spend 40 days in the desert in fasting and praying, preparing for the task ahead. Notice that Jesus does not do what the Pharisees of his time did: Put on a mournful and wasted look to announce to the world that they are fasting. Instead, Jesus goes to the desert where no one can watch him fast and pray. He will communicate with the Father and concentrate on his mission. At the end of 40 days, when his fast has ended, the devil tempts him – with seductions of pleasure, power and riches. Quoting Scripture, Jesus fends off the devil's attack. Then angels come to comfort him. We visit the Mount where Jesus was tempted, to remind ourselves of the lessons Jesus taught on battling Satan.

Reflection: Like Jesus do we undertake serious preparation before we commence an important task? Like Jesus do we fight temptation, with God's help, and drive the devil away, or make excuses for our frailty and succumb to the devil? As Peter wrote: The devil is a roaring lion waiting to consume the unprepared. We need the armor of prayer and the blade of firm resolve to defeat him. Never forget that the devil is a fallen angel, with more powers than we have. He will use falsehood, deceit and glamor to entice us. We cannot fight him on our own. We need help - God's help. If only we follow the example Jesus set us of chasing away the devil! *"On the day I called, you answered me." Psalm 138: 3*

CHAPTER SIX

The New Testament – the ministry of Jesus

"I delight to do your will, O my God, your law is within my heart." Ps. 40: 8.

Covering the ministry of Jesus is outside the scope of this book. Here, I attempt to cover only those sites we visited - that relate to his eventful ministry.

Mount of the Beatitudes: After his baptism – when he receives the Holy Spirit – and 40 days in the desert, Jesus begins his ministry. We notice that Jesus did not perform any miracles until he received the Holy Spirit. It is safe to assume that he was a conduit for the Holy Spirit and the Father. With his superior intelligence (Emotional and Spiritual intelligence) and inputs of The Holy Spirit he performs wonders that have both puzzled and edified the world.

Now, Jesus climbs Mount Tabor on the north-western point of the Sea of Galilee to announce his new law of love. The Beatitudes, so eloquently summarised in chapter 5 of Matthew's Gospel, can be summed up in the Golden Rule: *"In everything do to others as you would have them do to you" Mt. 7: 12.* The Golden Rule has found favour with other religions – Hindus, Muslims, Buddhists, Jews and others. Their holy books enshrine the Golden Rule, but in different words, with only Jesus defining the rule in positive terms. Mahatma Gandhi is known to have read the Beatitudes and gained an insight into the person of Jesus, whom he revered. A sanctuary commemorates the place where Jesus laid out his master plan. Expansion of the Beatitudes will call for a book, which I am not attempting here. May I recommend reading Mathew's Gospel, chapter 5, and Biblical commentary on the Beatitudes?

Reflection: The Ten Commandments, The Beatitudes, The Golden Rule are best paraphrased in the two commandments Jesus gave us: Love your God and love your neighbor. We have committed these to memory; now it is time that we commit to live them. We do not like to be hurt, but have no qualms in hurting others. We like to be in peace, yet we will not let others enjoy their peace, because we are planting seeds of dissension among opposing groups. And, our worst sin is our inconsideration of the spouse, children, parents and others at home. It is time for contrition and change!

The Lord's Prayer: Expanding on the Beatitudes, Jesus teaches his disciples and the crowds to pray (Mt. 6: 9-15). Most Christians recite the prayer, not pray it. If they did pray it, their lives would be different. It ranks first among all our prayers, because Jesus taught it. Rightly, the first part is on the will of God – which Jesus had come to fulfill. The line from Ps. 40: 8, that appears at the start of this chapter sums up his attitude to the Father's will. In the second part of the Lord's prayer, we have supplication for bread and forgiveness. The reference to bread is not confined to food, but all our needs – spiritual and temporal. And, his reminder on forgiveness emphasizes the reciprocal aspect of the virtue of forgiveness: forgive to be forgiven. It means chances of being forgiven are slim when we do not forgive others. The **Pater Noster (Our Father) Church** celebrates the Lord's prayer.

Reflection: When we pray the Lord's Prayer, do we pray from our hearts? We cannot move on until we have answered some questions. We pray for our needs, no doubt, but what is our disposition: one of trust or doubt? Do we insist on an apology before we forgive? Do we expect the offender to take the initiative? Do we keep score of the times we are offended? When we forgive others, do we also try to forget the pain?

Peter's House: Mt. 8: 14-17 recounts the miracles Jesus works at Peter's house. Jesus is never idle, always on the move, serving his fellows. Peter's mother-in-law is a quarrelsome woman, yet Jesus heals her of her fever and brings cheer to a crowd of ailing people who wait outside the house of Peter. At noon we have lunch at a restaurant that serves a dish called Peter's Fish.

Reflection: How eager and ready are we to reach out to those in need? Start with our homes. Do we touch our families with our hearts? Do our neighbors inhale the fragrance of our good deeds? In our work stations do our fellows see Jesus in us?

Jesus calms the storm: With crowds following him, Jesus decides to cross the Sea of Galilee. Tired from a hard day's work, Jesus sleeps in the boat. Soon a windstorm rises and sculpts the water into mountain-like waves. Despite knowing the sea well, the disciples are terrified. They rouse Jesus, in an accusing tone. Rebuking the wind, Jesus calms the storm, much to the amazement of his disciples (Mk. 4 : 35-41). What kind of man is he, they puzzle? Jesus visits the Sea of Galilee often, twice calming storms to rescue his disciples.

Reflection: What storms are we in? Is there danger that our boat will sink? Have we asked for help from Jesus – knowing that he never sleeps. He is the wonder-worker who never fails, when we trust him.

Sycamore tree: Lk. 19: 1-10 narrates the story of Zacchaeus. Short in stature, he climbs the tree to watch Jesus, who beckons him to come down, because he plans to stay with him that day. Zacchaeus is ecstatic. How could he a sinner welcome Jesus, the Son of God! He confesses his sins and promises to make amends to those he defrauded. In return Jesus promises salvation to him and his family. The narration gives us hope – when we repent Jesus takes us into his warm embrace.

A remnant of that tree survives. The hope of Zacchaeus is not dead – it survives in each of us who reposes our faith in the Lord!

Reflection: What tree do we climb to get a better view of Jesus? What efforts do we put in to stay connected with him? Like Zacchaeus, what are we willing to give up to gain his friendship? Love means sacrifice.

CHAPTER SEVEN

The New Testament – The last days of Jesus on earth

"By this everyone will know that you are my disciples, if you have love for one another" Jn.13: 35.

Upper Room: The Gothic architecture of this commodious room, in the southwestern corner of the city, on the first level, was modified by the Muslims, long after Jesus and his disciples met there for the last time, just before his passion and death. The alterations seem like a rude intrusion into serene ambience – although the main structure of the room is unchanged. The air of solemnity in the room nudges visitors to take measured steps, and to speak in whispers.

It is believed that the Upper Room stored the Ark of the Covenant, centuries ago, and that Nicodemus and Joseph of Arimathea, disciples of Jesus in private, jointly owned it. Jesus used the room – decorated for the occasion - the previous year also.

On the Passover, an important feast of the Jewish Calendar, Jesus invited the disciples to his last meal on earth. Much followed that significant decision to meet in the Upper Room:

- Jesus washed the feet of his disciples. Normally slaves performed this task. Here, Jesus, the King of Kings, bent low to wash and wipe the dusty and dirty feet of his disciples, urging them to follow his example. His example in humility would stir them to similar heroic deeds, stated in the Acts of the Apostles.
- He instituted the sacrament of Holy Orders – making priests of ordinary men; giving them the power to invite God to take abode in a piece of bread, and the power to forgive sins.
- He left himself behind under the veil of bread, so that man could receive him as food for the soul, until the end of time.
- Giving the disciples his farewell message, he asked them to love one another as he had loved them (Jn. 13: 35).
- He shared his last meal on earth with them. They would recall the solemn event, even as each of them went to a horrific death.
- After the death of Jesus, the terrified disciples would flee to the Upper Room, away from hounding Jews.
- The Risen Jesus would visit his terrified disciples to give them courage and strength; he would confront Thomas and his lack of belief in the resurrection.
- Days later, in the same room, the Holy Spirit would descend in the form of tongues of fire, on Mother Mary and the disciples. The Holy Spirit lifts their sagging spirits. Then they cast off their tattered garments of fear, to put on gorgeous robes of courage. The crowds who hear and see them are amazed.

These momentous events are recorded in Mt. 26: 17-35, Jn. 20: 24-29, Acts 2: 1-13.

Reflection:

- At the Last Supper Jesus summarized the Ten Commandments into two commandments: Love and serve God and our neighbor. How seriously do we take these commandments? How well do we observe them?
- Do we confess our sins and seek forgiveness of the Lord through the Sacrament of Reconciliation?
- Do we receive Holy Communion reverentially and frequently? What if our Churches were demolished and priests banned from celebrating mass, would we miss the Eucharist on our altars, and the sacrament of Reconciliation, in the confessional? Would the Lord's absence in our churches make us distraught? Do we realize how fortunate we are to have Confession and the Eucharist in our churches?
- Like the Lord do we wash the feet of others in serving them?
- Like Thomas, do we still doubt the Lord's word? Do we need proof? For those who believe, no proof is necessary. For those who don't, no proof is enough.
- Are we devoted to the Holy Spirit? Do we yearn to receive him in the sacrament of Confirmation? Does he make a difference to our spiritual lives? Do we sense his throbbing power?

Garden of Gethsemane: Gethsemane means oil press. Oil is pressed from olives that grow in plenty. The garden is across the Kidron Valley, and at the foot of the Mount of Olives. Stumps of olive trees, growing within a metal enclosure are old, some dating back 2000 years. The garden in its present state, gives us a glimpse of what it was 2000 years ago.

Mt. 26: 36-46 records the pain Jesus experiences in the garden, as he prays, weeps, bleeds and implores his disciples to pray. The agony is oppressive, the pain unbearable, and Jesus is heart-broken. Be still and listen to the heart-break of the Lord! Watch the first among men cry! The sins of the world, from the beginning of time pass before his mind's eye, as he prepares to pay the price for them. A God pleads with men to keep his company, but men will not – they sleep. Even in that state Jesus makes an excuse for them: the spirit is willing, but the flesh is weak.

The palpable tension in the scene is broken by Judas who arrives with a band of armed men. He greets Jesus with a kiss. Peter, in act of just rage, cuts off the ear of one of the men, whose name was Malchus, a servant of the High priest. Jesus reprimands Peter and hurries to heals the ear of Malchus. Despite his agony, humiliation and distress, Jesus is compassionate and reaches out to those in distress.

A grotto marks the holy site of the arrest.

The Basilica of the Agony, also known as the **Church of All Nations** (sixteen were involved in the church-building effort), calls to mind the fateful event. It stands at the foot of Mount Olives, near the Garden of Gethsemane. The Rock on which Jesus knelt – a memorial to his agony - is placed in the center of the Church.

Reflection: Have we mediated on the agony of Jesus in the garden? Sinless and blameless Jesus takes upon himself the sins of the world – our sins – to atone for them. His agony is so intense that the pores of his skin ooze blood, which trickle down his body and fall to the ground. We think much of any effort that makes us sweat. Spare a thought for Jesus whose sweat turned to blood. What was the extent of his agony! Can we do something for our Master to lessen his grief? Like Jesus who healed Malchus, would we ignore our pain and help others?

House of Caiaphas: Caiaphas was the high priest at that time, but his father-in-law was the influential retired high priest, Annas. Together, they chose to cross-examine Jesus. They test him with many questions, but Jesus chooses to remain silent. His silence baffles them. Then, Caiaphas arrives at a conclusion: It is better for one man to die than for a nation to suffer. The taunting crowd agree (Mt. 26: 69-75).

After the interrogation, they lead Jesus to a dungeon, in the basement, where he will be confined and tortured. Persecuted, insulted, and mocked, Jesus suffers the whole night, deprived of food, drink and sleep. They cleverly avoid hurting his face and parts of his body that will not be covered by his garment – as they persecute him. They hope to hide his tortured body from the eyes of Pilate, the Roman Governor, whom they will meet in the morning.

The **Church of Gallicantu** stands over what was once Caiaphas' house. In the Church a glass-top over the dungeon gives us a view of the horrors below.

Reflection: Spending the night in the company of ruthless ruffians, Jesus suffers excruciating pain. Except his face, they torture all parts of his body – sadism at its worst. Jesus does not complain, but suffers meekly, because of his cause – humankind must be saved. Do we give a thought to the humiliation and crippling pain he suffered for us? Do we shed a tear for our Master and Lord? Do we resolve to make good our promise that we shall sin no more?

Peter's denial: Just outside the house of Caiaphas another scene unfolds. Peter, terrified of torture and death, denies Jesus three times, as women recognize him. The more the women insist, the more vehement is Peter's denial. A Sculpture of Peter in denial mode recreates the scene.

Reflection: Like Jesus will we stand up for what we believe in? Jesus did not relent even when brutally persecuted. Can we suffer pain for his sake? Not only did he suffer pain of body, but abject humiliation and ridicule – taunts of the worst kind. Are we prepared for similar torments? We tend to accuse Peter of cowardice. What of us? He openly admitted to fear of torture and death but repented and returned to Jesus. Do we have the humility and love of Jesus to give up sin and turn to him? We are worse than Peter when we prefer vice to virtue, pleasure over penance, greed over temperance, and gratification over self-control.

Pilate: In the morning, after a horrifying night, Jesus is rushed to Pilate, because the high priest cannot condemn Jesus to death; only Pilate can. On the way, they change the charge from blasphemy to sedition – Jesus tried to make himself king, they contend. Sitting on his Judgement Seat, Pilate questions Jesus and finds that he is innocent. To gain time and find a way out, Pilate sends Jesus to Herod, since he had jurisdiction over Jesus' territory. Herod taunts Jesus and sends him back to Pilate, smelling a plot. Now, Pilate cannot wriggle out of judgement. His wife cautions him against condemnation of Jesus to crucifixion, but Pilate cannot withstand pressure the priests mount on him. Only Caesar is King, the usurper must be put to death, they demand. To stall for time and to instill sympathy in the crowds, Pilate tries different methods to release Jesus: a) he offers a trade-off between Barabbas, the traitor, and Jesus, but the crowds spurn the idea of a trade-off; b) he has Jesus flogged by soldiers, when chunks of flesh are torn off his body, but the people are confused when they see Jesus drenched in blood after the flogging. They shout: Crucify him. Why? Earlier they had seen Jesus confident and powerful. Now they see him helpless and weak. Earlier they saw the disciple around him. Now, with the fleeing disciples, Jesus seemed alone and friendless. Is he the same Jesus they saw until a few days ago, they ask, in dismay? Is he an impostor, they wonder? c) Pilate rationalizes with the crowds, but they refuse to see any logic, blinded by the Chief priests and elders, who are relentless in their purpose. When he finds that the people are instigated by the priests, and determined to put Jesus to death, Pilate washes his hands, as a sign of acquitting himself of guilt, and signs the death warrant. Now, Jesus is condemned to carry his cross to Calvary. His journey to Calvary is covered in chapter eight, where we follow the Lord on his pain-filled and horrific way of the cross.

The **Church of Flagellation** marks the spot of the scourging, where Jesus' body is reduced to a red mass of vibrating pain.

Reflection: Pilate is terrified at the thought of angering the emperor and displeasing the crowd, who were on the point of rioting. He did not want to lose his position as Governor. Therefore, principles suffered, and justice was compromised. Jesus would suffer, because he had no patrons to protect him, no one to stand up for him. He was born in poverty, lived in penury, and would die in adversity. If we were in the place of Pilate, what would we have done? Would fair play have a chance? Would justice be upheld? If we were among the people who witnessed the injustice, would we have acted differently? *"Man is born broken. He lives by mending. The love of God is the glue."* Eugene O'Neill

When we prefer power, honor, pleasure, and possessions over what is right, we join the Pilate league. When we taunt and ridicule others, we join the Herod league. When we are fickle and led by others in their evil designs, we join the league of the crowds. When shall we be ourselves – purpose-driven and committed to the Lord?

The Denial of Peter

"I do not know the man! And at that moment the cock crowed." Mt. 26: 74.

CHAPTER EIGHT

Via Dolorosa (Path of the Cross)

"God comes to us through our scars and our wounds, not our awards and our acclamations." Jane Fonda

I have had the opportunity of praying the Way of the Cross in many churches, but never experienced the solemnity of the spiritual exercise, as I did when our group prayed it in the Holy Land – a walk across 2000 feet.

The actual Way of the Cross of fourteen stations was started only after 1521. Before that it was a devotion covering only seven stations. Saint Francis of Assisi is known to have spread the devotion, more through example. Although groups walk the way of the cross on their visit to the Holy Land, the locals attach great significance to it on Good Friday, when they carry a cross behind the celebrant, and climax the devotion with the hymn that tells the story in soulful lyrics: **The Rugged Cross.**

1. **The first station: Jesus is condemned to death**

The irony is that the first station starts outside the Islamic school of El-Omariye. A dark metallic plate on the wall, marks the station, not the kind we have in our churches. Providentially, The **Church of the Condemnation and Imposition** of the Cross is nearby.

Reflection: Why did Pilate condemn Jesus to die? Why were the Jews whipped into a frenzy demanding his death? Why did Jesus submit to the unfair and cruel punishment? The short answer is that Jesus was obeying the will of God to atone for the sins of man. God the Son was obeying God the Father. God obeying God, because only God, in the form of man, could atone for the sins of man, against God. The long answer is that Pilate was spineless and sought the easy way out. He could incur the displeasure of Jesus at no cost to his position, but did not want to run the risk of facing the Emperor's anger, if the restive crowds rioted. The people, incited by the elders, were confused. Now Jesus did not seem to be what he was even a few days ago. They could not answer the questions that assailed them and weakly submitted to the elders, who threatened to excommunicate them from synagogues – a state worse than death, for most - if they sided with Jesus.

As we point fingers at Pilate and the crowds, let us ask ourselves: How frequently do we condemn others, sometimes without good reason? How often do we condemn infants to death, when we consent to abortion? Are we any different from Pilate and the crowds? If we had not sinned, Jesus would not have to die. Not just Judas and Peter, but each of us added to his agony. In return for the sacrifice Jesus made for us, what does he ask of us? Repent and reform so that we gain eternal bliss. Even when our sins are pitch-black, he forgives us, when we are contrite. His generosity is unmatched!

Prayer: My Jesus, my Master, forgive me for the excruciating pain I caused you. In your mercy, wipe out my sins with your precious blood, and give me the grace to conquer temptation. Give me the grace not to condemn others and act unjustly.

1. **The second station: Jesus accepts his cross**

The cross is not smooth or evenly shaped. Two rough logs are hurriedly put together – uneven humps and over-growth stick out, making it more difficult for Jesus to carry it. The cross-bar weighed over 80 pounds. But Jesus does not refuse to carry his cross, claiming innocence. No. Instead, he accepts it and carries it, even as he admonishes us to carry our cross and follow him. His journey on sore-feet – which were burnt the previous night - over uneven terrain, will take him to Calvary.

The second station, marked on the wall of the Church of the Flagellation, is just a few meters away from the first. It reminds us of the merciless flogging our Master suffered at the hands of brutal Roman soldiers. The heavy cross slows Jesus on his walk, but the soldiers prod him with blows and the sting of the whip. There is no respite for him. He stumbles on in pain, with blood flowing from his many wounds.

The first church on the site was built by the Crusaders in the 12th century. In 1903, the church was refashioned; and in 1927, completely rebuilt.

On Fridays, at 3 p.m. a procession winds its way through the alley and passes the Ecce Homo Arch, the place where Pilate points to the flogged and bleeding Jesus and hopes to evoke the sympathy of the crowds. *"Here is the man,"* he declares. But the Son of Man receives no sympathy; instead the slogans get more strident and the mood more aggressive. *"Crucify him,"* they shout back.

Reflection: How do we respond to crosses in our life? Like Jesus do we accept them or shove them away? Complain? Turn surly and accuse God? Recall that Jesus did not promise us an easy life, but one that would lead to never-ending bliss, when we carry our cross with love for him, and follow him. Ronald Knox put it aptly when he wrote that the cross is an "I" that is crossed out. When we blank out the selfishness, pride and attachments, we begin to understand the meaning of the cross.

Prayer: My beloved, thorn-pierced King, I salute you and prostrate in adoration. You are my God and my everything. Forgive me my transgressions. Time and again, I have resented the cross – not knowing your plan for me and not trusting in your Infinite wisdom. I have been ungrateful – not counting my blessings, only lamenting my crosses. Forgive me and give me a change of heart.

3. Third station: Jesus falls for the first time

He has not had a morsel since the Last Supper on Thursday; not a drop to drink. He has lost much blood and is dehydrated. The scorching heat of the day makes things worse for him. His endurance is giving way and he falls for the first time.

The ruthless soldiers do not give him a chance to be free of his cross. They whip him, until he can take the punishment no more. He staggers to his feet, picks up his cross and inches his way forward. There are some who weep for him; but most jeer him, roused by the religious leaders. There is no one to help Jesus. He is alone, in pain and much sorrow!

A Polish Church marks the spot.

Reflection: We fall many times in our journey of life. But we expect sympathy and a helping hand – which Jesus did not get. We fall when we sin. We fall when we fail in our duties. We fall when we do not reach out to others in trouble. Do we introspect? Is our conscience at peace? When we fall do we call to mind the fall of Jesus? Do we pray to him to give us the strength to rise and carry on? There is much to be done and little time left for it. There is no room for self-pity. Instead, we need to steel ourselves with a new resolve – like Jesus - to move forward.

Prayer: My Jesus, falling is not a disaster as long as I rise, ask your forgiveness, and try not to sin again. Lord, but I am weak. I am beset with many problems. You, who know and understand everything, come to my aid. Let me not stay down, but rise with your help – because your hand is always extended in forgiveness and mercy.

4. Fourth station: Jesus meets Mary, his mother

Picture them as their eyes meet. Mary recalls the time Jesus was growing up. She kissed every ache, cleaned every bruise, comforted him in every sorrow and wiped every tear. Now, she is helpless as she watches her grown son tortured and brutalized. She can only weep and pray to the Father. Through his looks, Jesus conveys to his mother what he told others: *Take up your cross and follow me.* The mother of God does not run away. She stands. Alone she must carry her cross, though John the beloved disciple tries to comfort her.

A chapel belonging to the Armenian Catholic Patriarchate and an oratory mark the place. The Eucharist is exposed in the Church and people congregate to adore the Lord.

Reflection: Do we feel the pain that Mary felt? Can we put ourselves in her place? What would happen to us if someone dear to us had to suffer like Jesus? Would we lose faith in God? Would we turn into foul-mouthed monsters? Rather, can we learn from Mary to face sorrow with fortitude? Can we commend ourselves to her care and beseech her to look upon us with kindness? Can we reach out to others in pain, comfort them and lend them some strength? How do we treat our mothers? Do we value all that they do for us, right through life?

Prayer: My Jesus, you saw a sword thrust into the heart of your mother. Yet, you did not accuse Pilate or your persecutors. Teach me, my Savior, not to accuse others for my sufferings or the sufferings of those I love. Help me to draw courage from you and your mother to submit myself to the will of God and look upon his promises with hope. Help me, my Master. On my own, I cannot do it.

5. **Fifth station: Simon of Cyrene helps Jesus carry his cross**

Jesus is showing signs of exhaustion, and the soldiers who do not want him to die before he reaches Calvary, get him some help. They coerce Simon of Cyrene, a visitor from Libya, to assist Jesus with the cross. Simon had no intention of being drawn into the drama being enacted. So, he tries to evade the task, but threatening looks from the soldiers force him into the ordeal. Then his eyes meet the tender eyes of Jesus and there is a transformation. He sees no hate, only love and mercy in those compassionate eyes. No longer does he rebel. Now he becomes a partner in the ascent to Calvary. His mind goes to his two sons, Alexander and Rufus. Would someone help them if they had to suffer, he agonizes? His heart melts. In turn, Jesus, is grateful to Simon for his act of mercy.

At the fifth station, the Franciscans have a chapel, the altar piece of which depicts Simon of Cyrene helping Jesus.

Reflection: Often I am beckoned to situations when I can help, but shrug away the opportunity. It is too much trouble. Why should I? I have no connection with that person. I could be inviting trouble by helping him or her. Now, let my thoughts turn to Simon. He could have bluntly refused, despite the threats from the soldiers, because he was a visitor, not a local. Perhaps, the soldiers would have found someone else to help Jesus. But Simon lets the angel in him win over the devil. From being a reluctant stooge, he becomes a willing collaborator. Jesus acts as a change-agent to awaken compassion in him. We do not know how he was rewarded, but what is important for us, who are making the journey with Jesus, is that we become cheerful givers. If everyone turned away from helping others, what would the world come to? If there were no Good Samaritans, would fallen people stay fallen? If I was in trouble and everyone moved away, how would I feel?

Prayer: My Jesus, like Simon, let me lend a shoulder to the wheel. Give me the largeness of heart to lift the heavy cross others carry. Help me to make life easier for those in my home. If I can put a smile on a face, never let me begin with a frown.

6. Sixth station: Veronica wipes the face of Jesus

Although the station recalls Veronica wiping the face of Jesus, the fact is that she was named Nike (some refer to her as Seraphia, a friend of Mary) and the towel on which Jesus imprinted his face, the Veronica. While many women weep, one fights her way past obstinate crowds and barricading soldiers, to come face to face with Jesus. She shares the pain of her Master. In a small act of kindness, she wipes his blood and spittle-stained face on a towel. Instantly Jesus imprints his face on that towel. She is astounded and the crowds gasp in wonder. He repays her kind act, with a memento that she will always cherish. We recall that Jesus seldom or never asked for favors. When he received kindness, he showed his appreciation in a remarkable way! Tradition has it that Nike was the woman whom Jesus healed of her twelve-year bleeding ailment, when she touched the hem of his garment.

A Greek Catholic Church marks this station.

Reflection: If we were among people on the Calvary-route, would we have had the courage to breakthrough and help Jesus in a small way – give him a sip of water, a morsel of food, wipe his face, or speak to him a cheering word? Imagine the plight of Nike, with the crowds hurling abuses and intimidating soldiers brandishing their weapons!

Are we selective in offering help to those in trouble – when it is convenient to us, when we are not in danger, when there will be no backlash? Is there a parent in need of help, but too self-respecting to ask for aid? Is there a child in distress, but tongue-tied? Is a neighbour taxed with problems, but reluctant to stretch out a hand? Can we help them without making them feel ashamed or embarrassed?

Prayer: My Jesus, you gave me opportunities to help others, but I did not profit from them because I felt threatened and inconvenienced. Please give me the spirit of Nike, to put my problems aside and reach out to those in tears - those who others refuse to help.

7. Seventh station: Jesus falls a second time

The way of his cross is becoming more difficult. His strength is draining from his body, even as the cross seems heavier. Jesus falls again. Although Simon of Cyrene is helping him, he finds the task increasingly difficult. Jesus is forced to rise, from the fallen position, since the soldiers will not let him rest even for a few moments.

Reflection: We fall, not twice, but many times. Do we hurry and rise through repentance? Or, do we let weakness and lack of resolve keep us in a sinful state? Jesus was prodded by soldiers to rise. We do not have such menacing foes to jerk us into action. We have the power of prayer and our determination – prompted by the Holy Spirit - to spur us. Jesus is watching us, as we are assailed by temptation. He will not stay idle, when we plead for his help. Jesus knows what it is to fall – not into sin, but take a fall on his journey to Calvary. He is wanting, willing and waiting to help us.

Prayer: My Jesus, I am weak, but you are strong. In my weakness, I fall many times. I do not want to stay fallen, but I cannot rise on my own. I implore you, my Master, to hasten to my aid and lift me out of my distress.

8. **The eighth station: Jesus meets the women of Jerusalem**

Sorrowing women line the route to Calvary. Some of them were healed, others had demons driven out of them and many were fed, when hungry. They wonder why the miracle-worker cannot work one for himself. They do not connect with the fact that Jesus never worked a miracle for himself – a miracle was always for others. Jesus understands their sympathy, but urges them not to weep for him, rather that they repent for their sins and reform.

Take up your cross and follow me, is his silent teaching to them.

The Orthodox Monastery of Saint Charalampus commemorates the station.

Reflection: How often am I not among those women who shed tears of sympathy - not empathy - for Jesus, but will not repent and reform? I am trapped in my sinful state. I rather worry over how my neighbors view me, how my colleagues assess me, and how my superiors evaluate me, not on how Jesus finds me – astray from his teachings.

Prayer: My Jesus, let me not just shed tears, but change my ways. Let me have the courage to follow you at all times. Let me understand your deep love for me and respond in love. Help me to value the things that matter and not hoard trinkets.

9. Ninth Station: Jesus falls for the third time

Calvary is within sight, but Jesus stumbles and falls for the third time. Perhaps Jesus fell more than three times, but only three are recorded. His fall showed how weak he had become and how exhausting the journey was. He had no escape; he had to finish the journey to the hill-top, where a horrifying end awaited him. The jeering crowds and tormenting soldiers only add to his misery.

The station is between an Ethiopian Monastery and the **Coptic Church of Saint Antony.** It is just a few yards away from the Basilica of the Holy Sepulchre.

Reflection: Jesus is resolute and courageous. He is full of love for us and will not let his weakness of body deter the purpose of his will, to complete his pain-filled journey. He will let nothing rob us of our redemption. Even as his body is wracked with pain, his mind turns to his disciples who had run away. Only John chose to follow him at a distance. Imagine the state of his betrayed mind! He is forsaken!

Prayer: My Jesus, when I am tempted to give up, please steel me with a firm resolve to carry my cross for your sake. Let nothing stop me from accomplishing my mission in life. Let me not look for human applause, but your approval from the cross.

10. Jesus is stripped of his clothes

The soldiers tear his garments – soaked in blood – from his badly wounded body. Flesh that adheres to his garment is torn from his body, opening wounds once more, to let blood gush from them. The pain is excruciating and Jesus lets a cry escape his parched lips. Imagine his humiliation as he stands naked before the vulgar crowd. The teasing gaze of the people freezes him. The two criminals who were to be crucified with him giggle as they disrobe. Quickly Mary sends her veil to Jesus, which Longinus, who oversees the crucifixion allows. Hurriedly and securely Jesus wraps himself with his mother's veil. Now he is ready for the worst. There is a notion among some that Jesus was crucified naked. It is not true. The fact that he was not naked is documented (Source: Poem of the Man-God by Maria Valtrota).

The **Chapel of Golgotha** is at this station.

Reflection: By permitting his clothes to be wrenched from his battered body, was Jesus atoning for our sins of the flesh? In our permissive lifestyle, where nakedness is not taboo – only joked at - we have lost our sense of sin. Some societies boast of their nakedness, other drop their clothes at the hint of pleasure. The sins of the flesh have become so common that no one frowns on them. They are in fashion. The sixth commandment is clear: Do not commit adultery with the opposite sex or same sex. Have our standards dropped so low that we do not recognize sin? Is our moral compass lost? Are we lost?

Besides our lust, what else can we strip from our minds and bodies? What about pride? Self-righteousness? Bloated egos? Selfishness? Vindictiveness? The list is endless. Shall we begin today, now, to rid ourselves of all that puts a distance between us and Jesus? As he stands naked for a short time, he reminds us that he gave up everything for us. What are we ready to give up for him?

Prayer: My Jesus, I have sinned and stand before you in shame. I have abused myself and others. My conscience is blunted and pricks me no more. Restore in me, my Merciful Savior, a new response, a new way of looking at sins of the flesh; at sin itself. Help me to shut the windows to temptation – my eyes that wallow in obscene sights and pictures, my ears that revel in dirty jokes and sordid details, my touch that rouses me to unpermitted sexual acts, my imagination that clouds my weak resolve to avoid sin. Blot out of me all traces of pride and vindictiveness, so that I can relate to others with love – even as you did. My Jesus, I am very weak. Please make me strong and clean me with your precious blood.

11. Jesus is nailed to the cross

Crucifixion was the most brutal form of Roman punishment. And, Jesus the spotless and blameless victim was to be crucified. Holes for the nails were already made in the cross. His right hand was stretched over one hole and a nail was driven in the part of the hand between the palm and wrist – not through the palm, as suggested in images of the crucified Christ. He lets a groan from the pit of his gut, escape his trembling lips. Then he hears the painful groan of his mother. Now, he will not add to her pain, so he silences himself. Even in his excruciating pain he thinks of others. His persecutors move to his left hand. The hole in the cross does not align with his hand. So, they tie a rope to his left hand and stretch it over the hole. The shoulder muscle is torn and the ligaments in his hand snap, adding to his pain. Yet they cannot get his hand aligned to the hole. With no option, they drive a nail through his left palm. On either side, nails clamp his hands differently. That done, they move to his feet. Placing foot on foot, they hammer a huge nail through them. Hands that blessed are pinioned to the cross. Feet that walked to teach and heal his people are now riveted to the cross. Now, they raise the cross, which swings violently. In one mighty heave they drop the cross into a pit prepared for it. The body of Jesus shudders as pain screams through it. For the soldiers it is fun of a different kind. But for Mary, John and the other holy women their hearts almost burst with pain as they watch their Lord and Master suffer the most horrific end. They will not run away. They will tell the Father to accept their pain.

Reflection: To reach Jesus, we too must climb the cross. To do that we must divest ourselves of earthly attachments – to money, pleasure, power and honor. Into what habits of my life should I drive nails? What wrong priorities in my life need to be riveted to the cross? What uncharitable thoughts should I pierce with the lance of penance? If we are led to tears, let us not stop them, but weep without restrain to mark our deep sorrow and repentance. He will forgive us, when we are truly sorry. The saints have found that meditation on the passion and death of Jesus is a sure way of increasing in holiness. Could we follow them?

Prayer: My Jesus, my sins nailed you to the cross. Without a word of protest, you carried the weight of my sins. How can I thank you, my Lord? You need no words, only a reformed life. Forgive me. Solemnly I promise to change, to give up my sinful ways and live your two commandments: love of God and neighbor. Help me, my Master, without you I can do nothing.

12.   Twelfth Station: Jesus dies on the cross

Lead-soled moments limp past. Jesus speaks to his mother, John, the thief on his right, and his Father. He knows that his life is being drained out, with each drop of blood that drips from his battered body. He forgives everyone – right from the beginning of the world to the end, including his persecutors, betrayer, denier, Pilate, the High priests, the soldiers and crowds who mocked him. Through John, he commends humankind to the care of his mother, and tells the disciple to care for Mary, now alone and unprovided. With his mission accomplished, he is ready to give up his soul to his Father. He dies. In a fit of anguish, the earth heaves a sigh, as rocks are hurled into the air. The curtain in the Temple is torn asunder – now man can speak to the Father directly and freely, not through the Levites. The dead are roused from their graves and walk the streets. Time stops, so to speak. This is no ordinary man who is dead. He is the Son of God and Son of Man. Tradition has it that the grave of Adam was near the cross. The blood of Jesus flowed to Adam's grave to make him the first fruit of redemption.

The **Chapel of the Crucifixion of Jesus** and the **Chapel of Calvary** are mute testimonies to the death of our betrayed Savior – betrayed not just by Judas, but by us, by our sins.

Reflection: Where can I run in my guilt? Will the mountains conceal me? Will the oceans cover me? My purpose is faulty as I try to hide. My thoughts are wrong as I try to run. I cannot run away from you, my Master, but to you. You will forgive me and restore me to your friendship. I need both your forgiveness and limitless love.

Prayer: My Jesus, I am a sinner, but a repentant sinner. You promised to make scarlet into white. Let me be white again. Let me be your child again. Thank you for dying for me.

13. **Thirteenth station: Jesus is taken down from the cross**

Nicodemus and Joseph of Arimathea take down Jesus' body from the cross and give his lifeless body to his mother. Her cries rend the air, as she looks to heaven in her pain. She will mourn, but not question God's will.

The station is near an altar dedicated to the Mother of Sorrows and the **Chapel of Saint Longinus**, the Roman who supervised the crucifixion of Jesus, who was later converted.

Reflection: He was born in a stable, 33 years ago, with only one purpose – to save humankind. When he was 12 he spoke of doing his Father's business. Now he had completed the task he set out to do. *"It is finished,"* he said.

Jesus – our Savior and truest friend - died a horrific death at the age of 33, in the prime of his life. Imagine that someone very dear to us dies at the age of 33 – when life is just beginning for him or her. Imagine the tortured life that person lived just before death. We would be in tears and mourn the passing for a long, long time. We would be disconsolate and afflicted beyond comfort. Years later we would recall that death in tears. But what about Jesus? Do we mourn his death? Do we feel pain? Do we shed tears? Do we recall his agonizing death often? Are we not guilty of double standards?

Prayer: My Jesus, you gave us everything, not holding back anything. Help us to follow your example by giving you everything. Take my mind, my will, my soul, my thoughts, my actions, my very life. Transform it all. Let it be yours – now and forever.

14. Fourteenth station: The body of Jesus is placed in a tomb

Followers of Jesus place his body – with 5455 wounds - on The Stone of Unction to prepare it for burial. They embalm it with over 100 pounds of myrrh , although just a few pounds would have been enough. Here was no ordinary man. So, extraordinary measures were in order. There was a new and empty tomb nearby which belonged to Joseph of Arimathea. Into that tomb, Jesus' body was lowered. He owned nothing in life. In death he uses a borrowed grave. Tear-stained faces circle his body, as groans escape their quivering lips, and a stone closes the tomb. A fragment of that stone is preserved in the church.

The Stone of Unction is under a massive dome in the church and near a **Chapel in honor of Nicodemus and Joseph of Arimathea.**

Reflection: The tomb is not the end of life – as Jesus showed. In three days he rose from the tomb to conquer sin and death, and pave a way for us to heaven. The shame of the crucifixion was eclipsed by the splendour of the resurrection.

Is my life sinking in the quagmire of failings and sin? Is my life a poor example for my children and others? What do I have to show for a life well-spent? All is not lost if I place my trust in Jesus and his Resurrection.

Prayer: My Jesus, there is more darkness in my life, than light. But you are the LIGHT. Let it pierce my darkness and show me the way to YOU. This I ask in the name of the Most Blessed Trinity. With the gates of heaven thrown open, guide me home.

CHAPTER NINE

Other Holy Sites

"The glory of God is a person who is fully alive." Saint Irenaeus

Jesus is buried; three days to go for Easter. The **Garden Tomb** is the place where he was buried, and from where he rose (Mt. 28: 1-5). The **Church of Saint Mary Magdalene**, managed by the Russian Orthodox Church, marks the place where Jesus appeared to her – a sinner turned saint; a reminder to us that we too can become saints. After his resurrection, Jesus appears to his disciples and others, to affirm his teachings, and instill hope in the dispirited. The **Rock** on which Jesus had breakfast with his disciples is placed in the **Church of Saint Peter**, which is nearby. During high tide, the waves of the Red Sea touch the compound walls of the church.

On the road to Bethpage, we head to the **Church of the Ascension,** on Mount Olives. The peak is 818 meters high and gives us a scenic view of the Old City. From here Jesus rose to heaven (Mk. 16: 19-20 and Acts 1: 6-11).

Later, we visit the **Tomb of Mary** – the site where the disciples placed the body of our Blessed Mother, after she died. Her sinless soul and body were then assumed to heaven. Two churches celebrate her Assumption – **The Basilica of the Dormition,** on Mount Zion, and The **Tomb**

of the Virgin Mary, near Gethsemane.

We also visited the **Qumran Caves** where the Dead Sea Scrolls were discovered in 1948. The Scrolls have led to much controversy – their origin being disputed. It is believed that in AD 68 (just before the Roman invasion) the Essenes, a monastic tribe, transcribed verses from Scripture on to scrolls and hid them in caves near the Dead Sea. The scrolls were discovered by a shepherd

Saint Jerome's Grotto reminded us of the saint who spent most of his life translating the Bible from Hebrew to Latin. His translation was the first step in making Scripture available in other languages.

CHAPTER TEN

Churches

"Don't shine so that others see you. Shine so that through you, others can see HIM." C S Lewis

The Holy Land is dotted with basilicas, churches, chapels, shrines, monasteries, convents, synagogues, mosques and a Bahai temple. It is no wonder that the place evokes sacred memories in Christians, Jews, Muslims and those of the Bahai faith. They all glorify God. There is a common feature in most of them: They are old, built in stone, in ancient architecture, dark, adorned with stained glass windows and beautiful domes. Most are large, some are medium-sized, and a few small. But all of them are sacred, solemn and sanctifying. Since we were rushing from site to site, we could not linger. But the experience gave us moments that turned to memories. We were fortunate to celebrate Holy Mass daily, at one of the churches, and receive the unequalled blessing of the Eucharist.

The churches we see today are not the original places of worship that the Romans built – mostly by Saint Helena, mother of Emperor Constantine - in the fourth century. Invasions, damage by fire, and destruction reduced them to rubble. Earthquakes took their toll. The Persians, and Turks, at different times, devastated what the Romans built. After the early destruction in the seventh century, the

Crusaders rebuilt some of the churches, which were soon brought to the ground by invaders. What stands today, at different sites, is the result of more recent reconstruction and refashioning – although remnants of the old are visible. All churches in the Holy Land do not find a place in this chapter – only the major ones. Not that there can be minor churches, because every church is God's temple. I refer to them as minor only in the context of less frequent visits to them by pilgrims. Such minor ones are listed at the end of the chapter.

The Franciscans played a major part in the restoration-projects. What strikes the visitor at these churches, is the quiet commitment of the custodians. They go about their duties with discipline, efficiency, solemnity and dignity. They – priests, pastors, monks, nuns and other clergy - are a marvel to watch and imitate. In a humble tribute to them, I have dedicated this book to the silent heroes.

In this section of the book, we shall briefly describe the churches at different sites and provide a little history, where possible. The names of the churches appear in alphabetical order. Some alphabets will be missing in the list, because churches with names starting with those alphabets were not built. As you visit the churches, try to connect with the notes you have here. Or, if you have completed your tour of the Holy Land sometime in the past, from these pages try to recall your unforgettable journey in the Lord's land.

A -1) Church of Saint Alexander Nevsky:

The church, named after a 13th century warrior prince, who battled against Sweden and Germany, is often overlooked because its façade resembles a hotel, not a church, although it is constructed in Baroque style, with red and white stones. It is built over the ruins of the Judgement

Gate – the gate through which Jesus passed carrying his cross. At the top of a stairway in the church is the depiction of Jesus carrying his cross. To enhance the effect, icons in gold and black decorate the church. The site is near the Holy Sepulchre Church and is known for its Russian Excavations. In front of the church is the Lutheran Church of the Savior.

A – 2) Church of Saint Anne:

The best-preserved Crusader Church in Jerusalem, marks the home of the parents of Mary, Anne and Joachim, and the birthplace of Mary. It is located about 50 meters inside the Lion's Gate, an important landmark in the city. The tranquillity in the church contrasts sharply with the bustle in the Muslim Quarter. Strong lines and thick walls give the church a fortress-like appearance. It is asymmetrical in design: opposite columns do not match, windows are of different sizes and buttresses differ in thickness and height. It is remarkable for its acoustics – even a small choir can sound like a large and gifted congregation.

The church was built by the Crusaders in 1140, and enlarged a little later. Providentially, it was not destroyed by the Muslims, but converted, by Sultan Saladin, into an Islamic Law School. Two or three centuries later, the building was abandoned. After the Crimean War, in 1856, the Sultan of Istanbul, who had control over that area, offered it to the French, in appreciation for the help they gave them during the war. The French restored the church that was in ruins. After the six-day war in 1967, between Israel and her neighbors, a second restoration was undertaken. Today it is regarded as the loveliest church - in Romanesque architecture - in that area.

The front of the high altar has three scenes: 1) The Annunciation, 2) Jesus being taken down from the cross, and 3) The Nativity of Jesus. On the left of the altar are illustrations of Mary learning from her mother, and her presentation at the Temple. A flight of steps descends to a crypt, that marks the spot where Mary was born. In the crypt is a small chapel dedicated to Mary. In the compound is a museum and a Greek-Catholic seminary. Next to the church is a large excavation of the Pool of Bethzatha, where Jesus healed a man unable to walk for 38 years (Jn. 5: 2-9).

Zippori is a slightly larger town, near the hometown of Mary. Scholars suggest that there was a large building being constructed in that place, where Joseph could have found work; with boy Jesus as his apprentice.

A – 3) Basilica of the Annunciation:

The Church reminds us of the visit angel Gabriel paid Mary to announce to her that she would be the mother of God – who would take human form. On the face of the building, at the top, is a bronze statue of Jesus. Below the statue is a relief of Mary receiving the good news from angel Gabriel. Below that picture is the one of the four evangelists, with appropriate verses from the Gospels and Isaiah – to put things in perspective. On the lower level of the two-storey structure is a grotto of the Annunciation. The church is topped by a 55- meter high dome. Today, the church which is managed by Franciscans, has about 7000-8000 parishioners.

A - 4) Church of the (12) Apostles:

Some refer to it as The Church Of the (7) Apostles – the seven who were present when Jesus met them after his resurrection (Jn. 21:2). It is located in Capernaum and managed by the Greek Orthodox Church. The Church celebrates Jesus choosing 12 disciples for his ministry.

What is important is that Jesus chose them; they did not choose Jesus, contrary to the practice at that time – of disciples choosing a Master. These disciples became Apostles, messengers, in the Acts of the Apostles – the part in Scripture that records the great deeds they performed.

After centuries of decay, the Church was rebuilt in 1931, and restored in 1969. It has two central domes, surrounded by six small ones, each topped by a cross, and painted in red. In the Church, frescoes and icons depict the crucifixion, resurrection, Mary and child Jesus, scenes from the Gospels, including the one on Judgement Day.

A – 5) Church of the Ascension:

Jesus accomplished his mission of redemption, through excruciating pain, a horrific death, glorious resurrection and amazing ascension. On the site is a church, managed by Russian Orthodox nuns who are known for the quality of their singing and icon-writing. Originally, the top of the church was open, to symbolize the act of ascending. Now, there is a dome that tops the church. It boasts of a 64-meter tower and a belfry with an 8-ton bell. A gap in the floor exposes a rock from which Jesus ascended to heaven. On Mount Olives, in an octagonal compound, the Church occupies the center, with the convent alongside. Outside the church wall is a rock on which Mary stood watching her son ascend.

The ascension of Jesus is celebrated at three other sites: 1) Dome of Ascension – a small octagonal structure, about 200 meters from the church. Now it is a mosque. A small building preserves the slab on which the footprint of Jesus appears. 2) The Lutheran church of Ascension, which is now a hospital for Palestinians. 3) The Greek Orthodox, Virig Galilaei ("men of Galilee") church is located between the Lutheran and Russian Orthodox Churches. We recall that the angels addressed the disciples as *"men of Galilee"*, when they looked up, stunned at the disappearing Jesus.

In 390 AD a pious Roman lady named Poimewa, built the first church on the site. That was destroyed when the place was over-run in the seventh century. In the 12th. Century the Crusaders rebuilt the church, which was also destroyed. What stands now was built in 1870. Hooks on the walls are meant to stretch tents that are put up during the feast of Ascension, when crowds congregate.

The church that celebrates the ascension of Jesus, has a connection with John the Baptist. It is believed that the head of John the Baptist was found by two Syrians monks in the fourth century. A chapel, in the compound, commemorates the spot. Thankfully, the Muslims acknowledge the ascension of Jesus. Therefore, Christians and Muslims celebrate the feast.

A - 6) Church of the Assumption:

It is located at the foot of Mount of Olives – across Kidron valley, just ahead of Gethsemane – and built by the Crusaders in 1130. It rests on the remains of the earlier churches built by Romans and others. Providentially, the church built by the Crusaders escaped destruction by the invading Muslims, since they also worship at this church in the belief that Muhammad saw a light over the tomb of sister Mary, during his night journey to Jerusalem.

Entry to the church is through the façade of the 12th century Crusader Basilica, that has been well-preserved. In the Church is a crypt and a niche dedicated to Mary, who was buried there, but assumed into heaven, body and soul. The assumption of Mary is authenticated in records of the early church. Near Mary's niche is another that is dedicated to Saint Joseph, her husband. Her tomb resembles that of her son, located in the Church of the Holy Sepulchre. The church is also known as the Dormition – or, the Basilica of the Tomb of Mary.

It has a conical roof and four corner towers. High above the altar is a mosaic of Mary with child Jesus, with a verse from Isaiah 7:14. The dome above the statute of Mary depicts Eve, Miriam, Judith, Ruth and Esther (women characters in the Old Testament). The upper floor of the church has a massive dome and mosaics. On the lower floor is a crypt where Mary is seen in a sleeping posture, reminding us of the last time her body was seen by the disciples. The statue was damaged during the 1967 war, but restored soon after. There is also a crypt marking the spot where Saint Helena found the cross of Jesus, in 327 AD. The church owns a fine organ, which is played on special occasions.

The management of the church is shared mainly by the Catholic and the Eastern Orthodox Churches. The Greek Orthodox, Ethiopian Orthodox, the Syrian Orthodox and Coptic Orthodox Churches have a small share in the arrangement.

Although there are claims that Mary was buried at the age of 64, in Ephesus, Turkey -where a house in which she lived is venerated - the evidence is clearly in favor of Jerusalem, where she is said to have died.

B – 1) Church of the Beatitudes:

Overlooking the Sea of Galilee, Tabgha – three kilometers from Capernaum – is the site for the church that reminds us of the Beatitudes – the sum total of the teachings of Jesus. Tabgha means seven springs – which water the fertile parcel of land. In 1938 the church was built over the remains of the Byzantine church. It was redone in 1982. Tabgha is also the site of the multiplication of bread.

The interior of the church is designed in clean, simple lines, to signify the simplicity of Jesus' teachings. An alabaster arch stands in the center of the Church, below which is the altar. Eight windows under the dome are of stained glass and bear the verses of the Beatitudes. The dome itself reflects light in a gold tone – to imply that the Beatitudes are nothing less than gold.

The high point in the history of that church are the visits paid by Popes Paul VI and John Paul II. They both celebrated Holy Mass there.

B – 2) Church of Bethphage:

Bethphage means house of early/unripe figs. The Franciscan-managed church, located on Mount Olives, Jerusalem, is close to Bethany, the hometown of Lazarus. It is the outermost point of Jerusalem – about 900 meters (3000 feet) from the city. Jewish Law permitted people to walk not more than 3000 feet on the Sabbath. Therefore, they could walk to Bethphage from Jerusalem to fetch baked bread, without breaking the law.

It is the place where Jesus looked for figs on a tree and found none. He let the tree wither to establish two truths: 1) Ask God anything in great faith and it will be granted. 2) Performance matters. Even the tree that did not produce fruit had no reason to live. We dread to think of what is in store for us when our lives are not productive.

It is the place from which Jesus started his Palm Sunday procession – with people cheering and applauding him. He knew how short-lived such applause was, because the same crowds shouted for his crucifixion a few days later. At the summit of Mount Olives, Jesus stopped to view his beloved city and lament its destruction in about 40 years – no stone on stone would be left. It is also the place where Jesus met Martha and Mary, before he raised Lazarus from the dead.

Commemorating many events at Bethphage, the Palm Sunday procession starts from there, and winds its way to Jerusalem. The Crusaders are known to have started the practice, that continues today. Bishops lead the procession, with children joining in large numbers to make the procession joyous and colorful.

In the church, above the altar is a mural of Jesus riding a donkey, applauded by crowds. On display, in the church, is a rock on which Jesus stepped, to mount the donkey. On the sides of the rock are paintings of the disciples fetching the donkey, people holding palm branches, and the resurrection of Lazarus – with the inscription "Bethpage". The arch in the Church was built in 1897 and the tower in 1954.

C – 1) Church of Saint Catherine of Alexandria:

The church has an engrossing tale to tell. Catherine, the beautiful lady had many suitors, chief of whom was Roman Emperor Maxentius. She refused his hand. To convince her of his good intentions, he sent her a band of fifty philosophers. When their discussions were over, the fifty were converted to Christianity. Infuriated, the Emperor had the fifty executed. Not content, he wanted Catherine tortured and killed. First, he had her thrown on the torture-wheel. Providentially, the wheel broke. When he missed the sadistic pleasure of watching her suffer at the wheel, he ordered that she be beheaded. Catherine was 18 in 305 AD – the year of her martyrdom. Tradition has it that angels carried her slain body to a hill near Mount Sinai, where it was buried. Later, her body was moved to Alexandria, where she belonged. The church houses her remains.

She was a soldier of Christ, who would not yield to the Roman-charm- offensive, preferring to die a cruel death. The story of her courage spread and many chose to emulate her by becoming Christians, prepared to follow Christ even under the threat of death. Recall that at that time Rome was against Christianity – so Christians were put to death. Her martyrdom was the high point in the history of the young church. For more reasons than one, her feast (November 25) is celebrated as a special day for unmarried women.

The church was completed in 1856 by the Franciscan architect Serafino da Baceno. A convent stands alongside.

C-2) Christ Church:

Resembling a synagogue, it is an Anglican Church that was built in 1849. It is the first Protestant church in the Middle East, and the first modern Jerusalem church to invite worshippers by ringing bells. In the early days it was known as the Jewish Protestant church, whose first bishop was a former rabbi – Michael Solomon Alexander.

The altar and stained glass windows display Jewish symbols and Hebrew script. The wooden screen behind the altar is a reminder of the Holy Ark, in which Jews of old kept the Torah. To stress his Jewish roots, the lineage of Jesus from King David, appears on a stained glass window. After much dithering, a cross was fixed on the altar in 1948 – to mark the place of worship as a Christian church. To cater to visitors, the church has a guest house alongside.

C – 3) Church and Monastery of the Cross:

At this site is a chapel, built in the 5th century, a monastery for the Greek Orthodox monks, a small museum, a gift shop and a coffee shop. Tradition has it that Abraham gave Lot three saplings of pine, cypress and cedar. Lot nurtured the plants with water from the Jordan River. The trees grew to be sturdy, handsome trees. It is believed that wood for the cross that Jesus carried came from one of those trees.

In the monastery, a circular plate marks the place where the trees stood. Frescoes from the 12th and 17th centuries adorn the walls of the chapel. Located outside the old city, the chapel and monastery have an important neighbor – the Knesset, the Israeli Parliament.

D – 1) Church of Dominus Flevit:

The church – built in 1955 by Italian architect Antonio Barluzzi – is tear-shaped to remind us of the tears Jesus shed over Jerusalem, as he stopped to view the city from the hill (Lk. 13: 34). Many times he tried to gather the people of the city like a hen that gathers her brood under her wings, but they would spurn his call. A mosaic at the foot of the altar shows a hen gathering her chicks under her wings, reminding us of the words of Jesus. Around the dome of the church are four reliefs representing scenes of Jesus' entry into Jerusalem. Viewed from the top, the layout of the church resembles a cross. A convent sits on top of the hill, not far from the church.

On the same site was a Byzantine church, built in the 5th century, dedicated to prophetess Anna (recall the presentation of Jesus at the Temple, when Simeon and Anna greeted the child Jesus and prophesied).

In the background of the church, rises the Grand Hasmonean Palace that served as the praetorium, from where Pilate condemned Jesus, and Herod's Upper Palace, boasting three enormous towers.

E – 1) Church of Ecce Homo:

It marks the place where Pilate addressed the crowds with the words: *Ecce Homo* (Behold the Man). Robed in purple, after the brutal flogging, Jesus wore a crown of thorns and was drenched in blood – a piteous sight. The crowds shouted: *"Crucify him"*. An arch, built in 1857, is meant to remind visitors of the cruel event. It replaced a structure that was a silent witness to the savage act of man, against his God, who had come visiting. The arch continues into a convent chapel. Pilgrims walk beneath the arch at the beginning of the Via Dolorosa (stations of the cross), recalling the passion and death of Jesus. A simply styled Catholic Church, managed by the Sisters of Zion, adds solemnity to the site.

Roman soldiers who idled, carved into the surrounding walls symbols of the games they played, leaving behind historic evidence, that is valued today.

G – 1) Church of Gloria in Excelsis Deo:
The church, managed by Franciscans, stands in the field where shepherds watched over their flock on Christmas night. Angels appeared to them to announce the good news. Since the field was only about 3 kilometers east of Bethlehem, the eager shepherds rushed to the cave to adore the King of Kings. They were reassured by the welcoming smile of Mary, and stayed for a time to watch in wonder.

The Shepherd's Field is cited in the Old Testament. Ruth gleaned wheat and barley in that field, in the company of other reapers engaged by Boaz. We recall that Boaz married Ruth – the ancestor of Jesus. Years later, David – an ancestor of Jesus – watched over his father's flock in the same place. Surely, the field was meant to go down in history as a landmark.

On the walls of the church are scenes from the Gospels – the appearance of the angels, the shepherds on their way to Bethlehem, and the adoration of the child Jesus. The translucent roof of the church allows light to stream in, reminding us of the heavenly light that bathed the shepherds.

J – 1) Church of Saint James:

The highly decorated church, built in 420 AD, and rebuilt in the 12th century, by the Crusaders, is located in the Armenian Quarter of Jerusalem. Armenia occupies a special status in Christianity since it was the first country to adopt it as the state religion, in 301 AD. Gilded altars, massive chandeliers, myriad lamps, paintings, carved wood, in-laid mother-of-pearl, bronze engravings and colored tiles embellish the church. Since it does not use electricity, high-set windows, oil lamps and candles are the only source of light in the church, which is open only during service.

The church is dedicated to two disciples of Jesus, with the name of James – the Great and the Less. James the Great was the brother of John Zebedee – the evangelist. James the Less was Jesus' cousin – on Joseph's side. James the Great became the first bishop of Jerusalem, but was beheaded by the grandson of Herod the Great, Herod Agrippa I. James the Less was thrown off the temple tower (the same tower that Satan took Jesus to during the temptations in the desert). Since James did not die from the fall, he was beaten to death. It is believed that the head of James the Great and the body of James the Less are buried in the church. Some scholars suggest that the site on which the church was built could have been Pilate's Praetorium – where Jesus was condemned. But there is no conclusive proof.

Across the street is the Armenian Orthodox seminary. In the compound is a museum with Armenian exhibits – art, culture, history and items of interest to visitors. The library next door, stocks Armenian literature and newspapers. Although the Armenians suffered at the hands of the invaders, their way of life is summarized in a slogan that appears at a local restaurant: *"From the unkind cup of history, they have drunk wisdom, not bitterness"*.

J – 2) Church of Saint John the Baptist:

It marks the place of John's birth. On the outer walls of the church, in many languages, are words spoken by Zachariah, in celebration of his son's birth (Lk. 1: 68 – 79), after his tongue was loosed. Ein Karem was about 6-7 kilometers west of the Old City and reserved for priests. Zachariah was one.

The church retains the style of the earlier ones. Restoration of the 5th century church was undertaken in the 17th century and 20th century. During the Crusade wars, the church doubled as a hospital for the wounded knights. After they recovered, they dedicated their lives to helping the sick. In the 16th century, it became a mosque, only to be returned to the Greek Orthodox Group. Next to the church is a monastery. The church is majestic with its tall tower, topped by a round spire.

J – 3) Church of Saint Joseph:

It celebrates Joseph's work place and the home of the Holy Family. The tomb of the Just Man in the church is believed to be the place where Joseph was laid to rest. Mary's well, nearby, is where Mary fetched water. In the family home Jesus spent 30 years of his hidden life. The church, also known as the Church of Nutrition, reminds us of the growing-up years of Jesus. Adhering to Jewish tradition, Jesus started his public life only at the age of 30; like David before him, who became King at 30, and Joseph, son of Jacob, who assumed major responsibilities in Egypt at 30. The church built by the Crusaders was laid waste by invaders, only to be rebuilt in 1914.

It is a good practice to revere a picture of the Holy Family in our homes, inspiring us to conquer ourselves, as they did: spreading goodwill, making sacrifices, encouraging a smile in those who sorrow, doing both pleasant and unpleasant tasks willingly and cheerfully, and inculcating a spirit of excellence in all that we do. These acts of love would set us on the path to holiness.

L – 1) Church of Saint Lazarus:

We know the oft-repeated story of Jesus raising Lazarus from the dead, four days after he was buried – when his body had begun to decay. What many might not know is that Lazarus was a very rich man, owning almost two-thirds of Bethany, his hometown, which was about 3 kilometers away from Jerusalem. The proximity to Jerusalem would have pushed up real estate value for Lazarus. Many of us might not know that Lazarus was ill and weak, and that his two sisters, Martha and Mary cared for him – Martha being the older of the two. When Jesus raised Lazarus to life, he returned to the sisters their beloved brother; they were overjoyed. The poor in Bethany rejoiced, because he was their benefactor. Generous to a fault, Lazarus helped the poor with cash and goods. Anyone could approach him with confidence. The strong support he received from the locals, besides his connections with influential people, was the reason Jesus and his disciples were safe at Bethany. No one would dare attack them in Lazarus' home. Perhaps his charity, fair-mindedness and friendship with the King of Kings earned him sainthood. On many occasions Jesus and his disciples were guests at the home of Lazarus, when Martha cooked and Mary listened to Jesus' teachings. On Palm Sunday evening also, Jesus retired to the home of Lazarus.

The church at Lazarus' tomb was built in 1954. A mosaic in the church shows Jesus meeting Martha and Mary before raising Lazarus from the dead. To symbolize the contrast between life and death, the dome in the church creates a fitting counterpoint of brightness and darkness.

The entrance to his tomb is reached after passing a mosque and a church. From that entrance 24 steps lead to a hall. From the hall more steps lead to the burial chamber. We recall that Jesus asked that the big stone be removed from the entrance of the cave, before he called out to Lazarus. At first he took unsteady steps; then firm ones to come out of the cave. He was alive! Here was a case of resurrection of the body. It reminded the assembled Sadducees that their denial of the resurrection was folly. What is more important is resurrection of the soul to rejoice eternally!

M -1) Church of Saint Mark:

The church, managed by the Syrian Orthodox denomination, is home to the smallest Christian community in Jerusalem – about 600 members. It is located in the north-eastern corner of the old city's Armenian Quarter. Services are in Syriac, which is a dialect of Aramaic – the language that Jesus spoke. Like most other churches described in this section, it was destroyed, but restored in 1940. A notice at the church declares that the original church was the first church in Christianity; therefore, there is much tradition in it. The inside of the church is dark, to symbolize its dark and troubled past, but decorated ornately to instill hope, and convey goodwill.

The oriental orthodox church – otherwise known as Jacobite church – derives its name from a bishop. It was separated from mainstream Christianity in the 5th century, over a dispute on the nature of Christ. They are not in communion either with Rome or Constantinople.

Saint John Mark was from Cyrene in Libya. In the Gospels we notice that there was another person who hailed from Cyrene; he was visiting Palestine at the time of Jesus' passion and death – Simon of Cyrene, who helped

Jesus carry the cross. He was reluctant at first, but gladly shared the burden of the cross once he looked into the face of Jesus. John Mark, challenged in one hand, was the traveling companion of Saint Peter. It is speculated that he was one of the 72 disciples Jesus chose in a second hiring process, after he trained the 12 – chosen the first time.

M – 2) Church of Saint Mary Magdalene:

The past life of Mary Magdalene is one of intrigue and sin. She was a known offender, a prostitute, who tried to seduce even Jesus. She operated from a place known as Magdala, now called Migdal. With her Roman friends, she joined the crowds who were listening to Jesus. Her friends challenged her to seduce Jesus. She accepted the challenge and did her worst with her flashing, bright eyes, tossed up black hair, and supple body to entice Jesus. Jesus looked at her compassionately, and switched from his subject to adultery, and continued to speak with the crowds. She was mortified and ran away giggling derisively. Later she was drawn to his words and actions and pondered her sinful life. With compassion for her, Jesus exorcised seven demons from her (Source: The Poem of the God-Man, by Maria Valtrota). Her conversion gives sinners like us much hope. If she can change, so can we. Because of her great love for Jesus she gave up her sinful past to follow him and his disciples on their travels. She was known to financially support the group, because she had money – accumulated from her truant ways. In a tribute to her, Jesus chose to appear to her after his resurrection – establishing that he had come to save sinners and not for those who were just.

She roused Peter out of his despondent state to beg Jesus for forgiveness, and resume his role as leader of the disciples. When the disciples – men - were hiding behind closed doors, for fear of the Jews, Mary Magdalene – a woman - dared to run errands for those gathered in the Upper Room. She was the second sister of Lazarus. Much of his ill-health was ascribed to his sister, and her sinful ways. But he rejoiced at her conversion and was deeply grateful to Jesus for making it possible. With God all things are possible!

The church, managed by the Russian Orthodox group, is located in East Jerusalem, near the Garden of Gethsemane. It was built by Tsar Alexander III in 1886. The location of the church is significant, because Mary saw Jesus after he had risen, near the garden. The Tsar ensured that relics of two Russian martyrs – Grand Duchess Elizabeth Feodornova and her fellow nun Varvara Yakovlena – were displayed in the church.

M – 3) Church of the Multiplication:

Tabgha, the location of the church is beautiful and tranquil. We recall that Jesus and his disciples retreated to this quiet place after receiving news of the death of John the Baptist. But the small group could not rest, because crowds followed them, even to this retreat. Jesus took compassion on them and taught them. In the evening, Jesus challenged his disciples to feed the crowd. They were dismayed. How could they? Even if they had money, which they did not have, it would take much money to buy bread for so many. It would mean carting heavy baskets of bread across a distance, because Capernaum, the nearest town was some distance away. Jesus knew what he would do. He told his disciples to let the crowds recline on the grass. Then he blessed 5 loaves of bread and 2 fish, which a boy in the crowd had. In contrast to those in the crowd who did not share the food they brought with them, the boy was prepared to share what he had. The Gospels do not refer to any money being paid to the boy. It is safe to assume that he gave his share of food for no money. He was generous. Jesus multiplied his generosity many times. The Gospels report that there were about 5000 men. Reckoning with women and children, it is estimated that more than 10,000 people were fed on that day. By using meager resources, Jesus teaches us not to despise small resources, which can multiply many times, when used judiciously. The untold miracle is that the multiplication pre-figured the Eucharist, which is food for our souls and divinizes us.

After the crowds had eaten, the disciples collected 12 baskets of left-overs, teaching us not to waste God's gifts. Every day we waste food at our tables. Think of the food wasted daily at restaurants. If only we fed the hungry with food that we waste, more people would go to bed in gratitude. In a way, the 12 baskets symbolized the 12 tribes of Israel and the 12 disciples, who were commissioned to feed God's word to the world. Each of us has a commission to feed others with the Word of God. How sincere are we in carrying out our mission?

Under the altar of the church is the stone on which Jesus placed the 5 loaves and 2 fish. The first church was built sometime in the 4th century by the Byzantine Romans. The church now standing on the site is a copy of the church rebuilt in the 5th century. On the altar is a mosaic of loaves and fish. Some mosaics in the church picture plants and animals to give us the setting for the miracle. The church is near three others – the church of the Beatitudes, the church of the charcoal fire, the church of the Primacy of Peter. We cover the Church of the Beatitudes in this section, but do not cover the Church of the charcoal fire, where Jesus served breakfast to his disciples who were tired and famished after fishing the whole night without success. At his command, they fished gain to take in a big haul. He had risen from the dead a few days ago. Now he was raising his disciples to a new level of faith. The Church of the Primacy of Peter commemorates the elevation of Peter to Head of the Church – the pope. Let us reflect, for a moment, on the meeting between Jesus and Peter after the denial. Not in word or action does Jesus accuse Peter. There is only forgiveness and restoration to his position as head disciple. Now, let us think of how we respond to those who offend us? We must give them a *'piece of our mind'*, *'put them in their place'* and relish the smug satisfaction of coming out on top. How different are our styles!

Near the church is a highway, where Matthew could have had his tax-booth, which he left to follow Jesus.

The Gospels alert us that Jesus performed a similar miracle, not far from this spot, when he fed 4000 men plus an equal number of women and children, with little or no starting material. The place was called Dodecathronon , now known as Tel Hadar.

N – 1) Church of all Nations:

It is also known as the Basilica of the Agony, completed in 1924, through the concerted efforts of 12 nations: Argentina, Belgium, Brazil, Canada, Chile, England, France, Germany, Italy, Mexico, Spain and the USA. Besides the 12, Hungary, Ireland, Poland and Australia made significant contributions – but their numbers are not added to the 12 nations who led the project. The original 4th century Byzantine church was destroyed by an earthquake in 746, and the 12th century Crusader-church was abandoned in 1345.

The church, located at the foot of the Mount of Olives, is built over the rock on which Jesus prayed the night before he was crucified. A grotto in the church, about 190 square meters, shows the spot where Jesus and his disciples stopped to pray. While Jesus prayed, the disciples slept, even as the Olive trees stood in mute testimony. The scene is evocative, as we contemplate the loneliness of the Lord. Meditating on the agony of Jesus can impact us, more than any book, homily or movie.

The church blends Roman and Eastern architecture, cleverly interposed by Italian architect Antonio Barluzzi. He left the interior of the church in semi-darkness to replicate the scene of Jesus' agony. The domes are in sombre blue to capture the night sky. The rock is placed in front of the high altar. The mosaics in the church picture: 1) The kiss of Judas 2) Jesus in agony, being consoled by angels 3) The arrest of Jesus. Some more mosaics that were unearthed during the 1924 construction are preserved under glass, on the floor.

On the facade of the church is a triangular mosaic depicting Jesus as the mediator between God and man; another portrays the four evangelists. On top of the church are two stags. Over the main altar, Jesus is shown in a praying posture. Over one of the side altars is a painting of the Assumption of Mary. Beneath the main altar are bronze figures of the sleeping disciples. The basilica has 12 beautiful mosaics representing the 12 nations who collaborated in building the church. In front of the church are 3 arches supported by pillars. The windows in the church are adorned with violet glass. The ceiling is embellished with 12 domes – representing the 12 nations. The rock where Jesus prayed and the grotto to mark the spot of his arrest, are only a dozen yards apart. In the garden of the church is an altar used by different Christian denominations.

N – 2) Church of the Nativity:

Joseph and Mary were visiting Bethlehem, 10 kilometers from Jerusalem, for the census, when it was time for the baby to be delivered. She laid him in a manger, in a cave, because there was no room for them in the inn. In 326 AD, Saint Helena commissioned a church over the cave, where Jesus was born. In 530 AD the church was enlarged. In the12[th] century the crusaders redecorated the interior of the church. In 1847 the silver star, placed in the church in 1717, marking the spot of Jesus' birth, was stolen, but found. On it was inscribed: *"Here Jesus Christ was born to the Virgin Mary"*. The 14-point star represented the star that guided the wise men to Bethlehem. Among other reasons, the stealing of the star was one that led to the Crimean War in 1854-56. Replacing the old manger, with one made of silver, did not gain favor with Saint Jerome, who spoke and wrote on the poverty in the life of Jesus.

The present church, considered to be the oldest Christian church still in daily use, restored in 2013, has an octagonal floor plan. It is 54 meters long, and is bare, with no pews, to symbolize Jesus who gave up everything to save us. In the center of the church is a 4-meter-wide hole, with a railing, through which the cave can be seen. The doorway to the church is only 1.2 meters high – urging visitors to bend low, as God did when he became man. The Persians spared the old church from destruction in 614 AD, when they saw a mosaic depicting the three wise men in Persian attire.

Remnants from the old churches are on display in the new church which is managed by Greek Orthodox Christians. They celebrate Christmas on January7, not December 25.

P -1) Church of the Pater Noster:

It is the place where Jesus taught the Lord's prayer, the Our Father, to his disciples. The Gospels refer to two occasions when Jesus taught the prayer – Mt.6: 5-15, in Galilee, and Lk.11: 1-14, when Jesus was on his way from Galilee to Jerusalem, prompting Bishop Eusebius (280-339 AD) to write: *"In that case the Savior of the universe initiated members of his guild in ineffable mysteries"*.

The first church on that site was built by Saint Helena. It was known by other names: Church of Eleona (Greek, for Olive Grove) and Church of the Disciples. Now the name Pater Noster has come to stay. This church was rebuilt in 1874 by an Italian lady – widow of a French Prince. When the church and convent were being constructed, the lady lived in a wooden cabin on the campus, to closely oversee the work on the church. She put up 39 translations of the Lord's Prayer – her favorite prayer - to attract visitors from different countries. She died in 1889 and was buried in the church. Today, there are 70 translations of the prayer on the walls. A gift shop on the campus sells postcards of the prayer in different languages. During the excavation they found a Latin translation of the prayer. They also found 2 mosaics with the words of Ps. 121: 8 and Ps. 118: 20.

In 1911 archaeologists discovered , then in a collapsed state, the cave where Jesus taught the prayer.

P – 2) Church of the memorial of Saint Peter:

It commemorates the place where Peter lived. It is octagonal with 8 pillars. An opening in the floor of the church, gives the visitor a view – at a lower level - of what was once Peter's dwelling. Near the church, in Capernaum, is a synagogue, where Jesus performed miracles. The synagogue measured 23 X 17 meters, with some stones in its foundation, weighing 4 tons.

P – 3) Church of Saint Peter in Gallicantu:

Gallicantu, in Latin, means "cockcrow". The church, located on the eastern slope on Mount Zion, is built over the house of the chief priest, Caiaphas, where Jesus was taken by the mob, after his arrest. It was at this place that Peter denied Jesus three times: *I do not know him.* On the roof of the church is a golden rooster to remind us of the prophesy Jesus made on Peter's denial. The site is also a powerful reminder of Peter's repentance and conversion, just the opposite of Judas' self-pity and refusal to repent. The 4 Gospels record Peter's denial, whereas 3 report on his conversion.

Under the church is the dungeon where Jesus was detained and persecuted on Holy Thursday night. It is dark and foreboding, and warns of hidden dangers, which Jesus discovered that night. The guardroom and dungeon have chains to fasten prisoners and bowls to hold salt and vinegar, to aggravate pain or disinfect wounds.

The building has four levels. On the upper and middle floors are churches. On the lower floor is the guardroom. And the dungeon is at the lowest level. In the courtyard is a statue of Peter in denial mode. A woman beside him, vividly brings to mind the scene of that night. The original church was destroyed and rebuilt in 1932 and renovated in 1997. Near the church is a flight of steps that Jesus walked on the evening of his arrest. His disciples had fled and he was totally alone and in great distress. Excruciating pain was to follow.

There are two Byzantine Era mosaics, uncovered during excavation, that are on display in the church. Besides, there are 3 large mosaics on the walls: 1) The last supper, 2) Jesus being arrested, 3) Peter in papal vestments. In the church many inscriptions are in French, since a French Religious Order, built the church. A huge cross-shaped window, in the roof, lets in light.

R – 1) Church of the Redeemer:

It is a Lutheran Church built in 1893 by Kaiser Wilhelm, of Germany – the newest church in the Old City. It boasts of a 48-meter high tower that conceals 177 steps to the top. From the tower a large part of the city can be seen. Viewing a rainbow icon is the highlight of the tour of the church. Above the entrance of the church are two Greek alphabets: Alpha and Omega – to symbolise God's eternity, with no beginning and no end.

In the garden is a memorial to the headquarters of the Crusaders – the Order of the Knights of Saint John.

R – 2) Church of the Resurrection:

It is also known as the Church of the Holy Sepulchre and church of Anastasis. It marks the site of his crucifixion – Calvary and Golgotha – and his tomb. Rightly, the last five stations of the way of the cross are prayed in the church, not in the open.

The first church was built by Saint Helena in the 326 AD. Emperor Constantine instructed Bishop Macarius, who oversaw the project, to make the church *"the fairest of all"*. In 614 AD the church was reduced to ashes, by a fire started by the invading Persians. An earthquake in 746 AD made things worse. In the 12th century(1149), the Crusaders rebuilt the church that was destroyed by Muslims in 1009. In 2016 the final reconstruction work was complete. At that time they discovered the remnants of an ancient tomb behind its ornate walls. Even today, the church bears scars of its turbulent past – fires, earthquakes and invasion, but two domes of the Basilica – one bigger than the other – stand out on the skyline of Jerusalem. It houses more than 30 chapels, giving it a crowded and gloomy look. However, it is the favorite spot for tourists.

Scenes from the life of Jesus – including his infancy, triumphal entry into Jerusalem, and the Last Supper – adorn a small Coptic Orthodox chapel in the church. In the church is a stairway leading to Calvary. On the ground floor are relics and a fragment of the Holy Cross, on which Jesus died. Just near the entrance of the church is the Stone of Anointing – where the limp body of Jesus was laid and embalmed before his burial.

The Protestants claim that another place marks Calvary. They point to a tomb in an alley, off Nablus Road, north of Damascus Gate. This site was unearthed in 1867. It is a tranquil spot, suited to prayer and meditation. However, there is more evidence that the Church of the Holy Sepulchre is in the right spot.

Some Christian Churches – Catholic, Greek Orthodox and Armenian Orthodox - warily share the management of the church, each claiming portions of it. At one time the keys of the church were entrusted to a Muslim family; not anymore.

S – 1) Church of Stella Maris:

It is also known as the church of Eli- Mukhraka. It is located on Mount Carmel, which is a limestone mountain range, stretching from Samaria to the Mediterranean Sea – about 25 kilometers long and 10 kilometers wide, with an average height of 500 meters. It is rich in water, vegetation and is dotted with caves – about 1000 of them.

In 1 Kings 18 we read of the test Prophet Elijah set King Ahab and his 450 false prophets and priests. Elijah triumphed because his offering was consumed by fire from heaven, whereas the offering of the false prophets and priests, despite repeated prayers to Baal, was untouched. In one simple test he demolished the claims of the pretenders, and established the power of the one true God.

The church – 70 meters long and 36 meters wide - built in 1836, commemorates Elijah's victory. Outside the church is a statute of the prophet. Inside the church are images of Elijah and other prophets.

The church is known as Stella Maris (Star of the Sea) because the Carmelite Religious Order was born there. The statute of Our Lady of Mount Carmel is placed near the cave that Elijah is believed to have occupied.

Mount Carmel is also sacred to followers of the Bahai Faith. The Bahai World Center and the shrine of Bab are located there. Bab, a key figure in the faith, was laid to rest in the early 20th century. The majestic super-structure boasts of an intricately-designed Golden Dome, decorative terraces, and beautifully laid gardens, at different levels. Visitors are not allowed to all levels of the gardens. The shrine and its surroundings are regarded as the religious head- quarters of the Bahai Faith.

T – 1) Basilica of the Transfiguration:

Mount Tabor is about 9 kilometers from Nazareth and about 558 meters above sea level. It is south-west of the Sea of Galilee.

In the Old Testament the story is told of Judge Deborah and Barah, her commander, defeating the forces of Sisera, the opposing general of the Canaanites. It was at Mount Tabor that torrential rains stopped chariots of the enemy, to give the Jews victory.

In the New Testament, at Mount Tabor, Jesus is transfigured to the amazement of his disciples – Peter, James and John (Mt. 17: 1 - 8). Jesus' visitors, at that time, were Moses and Elijah. In awe, Peter declares that it would be right if they put up three tents for Jesus, Moses and Elijah. To add to their wonder they hear the voice of God the Father: *He is my beloved Son. Listen to Him.* Shall we search our hearts? Do we listen to Jesus? If we did, we would be more Christian, perhaps saints. The disciples cannot explain all that is happening. They are wonder-struck and speechless. Centuries later, what does the transfiguration of Jesus mean to us? Do we honor and glorify the Son of Man and Son of God? Do we see Him as an indivisible part of the Holy Trinity? Do we pay homage to him as the King of Kings? Are we proud to be his subjects? Are we one with him in his glory and abject humiliation?

The original church was built by Saint Helena, which was destroyed by the invaders, at different times. It was rebuilt in 1924. The Greek Orthodox and Catholics – Franciscans – share responsibility for managing the church, which has two towers representing Moses and Elijah.

Not far from Mount Tabor is a place called Nain. The Gospels report a miracle that Jesus works there. The only son of a poor widow is dead. Jesus halts the men carrying the body of the boy, and raises him from the dead, to the wonderment of the crowds and relief of the widow. Her only hope is alive once more! As always, Jesus empathizes with the distressed and heavily-burdened, and destitute women.

V – 1) Church of the Visitation:

It is the place at which Mary met her cousin Elizabeth. At their meeting, the child in Elizabeth's womb leaped for joy. At that moment, the Holy Spirit cleansed the child of the ill-effects of original sin. On the walls of the compound, in over 50 languages, the Magnificat (Lk. 1: 46 – 55), Mary's song of praise appears. On the wall of the church is a mosaic that depicts Mary journeying on a donkey to Ein Karem from Nazareth – protected by a host of angels. Fittingly, a sculpture of Mary and Elizabeth in close communion, adorns the outside of the church.

Inside the church are paintings and mosaics celebrating Mary: at Cana, protecting the faithful with her mantle, and her divine motherhood. The dome of the church is supported by 4 pillars. In the dome are 8 windows, painted silver on the outside. Over the earlier constructions, the Franciscans completed the present church in 1955.

W – 1) Franciscan Wedding Church:

It is also known as the church of Saint Bartholomew, Jesus' disciple, who belonged to Cana - which is 5 miles north-east of Nazareth. Weddings and wedding anniversaries are celebrated at this church, because of its history. In its vicinity, shops sell Cana wine, tempting visitors to buy bottles of wine before they return home.

Nearby is the Greek Orthodox Church of Saint George. In it is a mosaic map of sixth century Israel, that adorns the floor. The fine detail in the map is amazing.

Jn. 2: 1-11 recounts the first miracle Jesus performed. His mother and his disciples were also invited to the local wedding. Although Jesus was busy, he was never harried to refuse an invitation to a wedding, where he would meet people, and people were his concern. When wine ran out, Mary asked her son to help out. It is good to recall that Jesus performed his first miracle at the behest of his mother, reminding us that her intercession is important. Her words to the servants are words of caution to us: *"Do whatever he tells you"*. Are we doing what the Lord tells us to do? At Mary's request Jesus advances his time to perform miracles – he was now starting his public ministry.

Imagine 350 liters or 730 bottles of wine, suddenly available to the wedding party! In one stroke, Jesus gave them a huge gift of wine and sanctified their wedding. The Divine Alchemist was at work! The sacrament of matrimony had a joyous start! It is time for us to ponder: Are we living sanctified married lives? Does our example edify other couples? A wedding is a sign of giving one to the other in an act of love. Jesus, the eternal sign of loving and giving, sanctifies each wedding that trusts in his saving power.

During the excavation in 1879, they discovered a synagogue below the ancient church. The rebuilt church has two levels, and two bell towers. At each level, a chapel is the highpoint. One of the jars, used in the miracle, is preserved in a museum, located opposite the Greek Orthodox church of Saint George. Also dummy cisterns, that resemble the original are exhibited.

What is Jesus teaching us, when he transforms water into wine? That we, ordinary people, can be transformed into his extraordinary followers, when we place ourselves into his wonder-working hands. Are we ready to let go of money, possessions, relationships, to take his hand?

By listening to Mary, not only is he seen as an obedient son, but also as God himself who would heed his mother's intercession. How fortunate we are to have Mary as our advocate! Is the rosary, dear to her, an essential part of our family prayer? While on the subject, we should counter the false propaganda of some Christians that we worship Mary. WE DO NOT WORSHIP MARY. Worship is due only to the Creator, not creature. But we honor her and pray to her that she intercede on our behalf with her son. That the Lord listens to his mother is proof of her power – which comes only from him. Mary is God's mother. Therefore she is venerated.As humans we love and care for our mothers. How much more would God not love and care for his mother, where no son loved his mother more than Jesus, and no mother loved her son more than Mary!

Some of the minor churches in the Holy Land:

1. A Catholic Church dedicated to Joseph of Arimathea and Nicodemus, followers of Jesus, who arranged for the burial of Jesus.
2. Church of Saint Onuphrius – Greek Orthodox built in 1874 – on the Field of Blood. Above the main door of the church is a picture of the Saint bowing to an angel. The plot was bought with 30 pieces of silver that Judas returned to the priests, when he felt some remorse for his act of betrayal. Since the clay of the land was good, potters used material from there to mold their pots. Later, the place was set aside for burying strangers. It wears a deserted and forsaken look.
3. Church of Our Savior the Illuminator, built over the Pool of Siloam. Destroyed in 614 AD.
4. Church of the Charcoal Fire, near the beach, where Jesus hosted breakfast for his famished disciples, after his resurrection.
5. Church of the Condemnation and Imposition of the cross – at the first station of the cross.
6. Church of the Flagellation – at the second station of the cross.
7. A Polish Church at the third station of the cross.
8. An Armenian Catholic Church at the fourth station of the cross.
9. A Franciscan Chapel is built at the site of the fifth station of the cross. The altar piece shows Simon of Cyrene helping Jesus.
10. A Greek Catholic Church near the sixth station of the Way of the Cross.
11. A Franciscan Chapel near the seventh station of the Way of the Cross.

12. An Orthodox Monastery and Church of Saint Charalampus near the eighth station of the Way of the Cross.

13. The ninth station of the Way of the Cross is between an Ethiopian Monastery and the Coptic Church of Saint Antony. Just a few yards away is the Basilica of the Holy Sepulchre.

14. The Chapel of Franks, also known as the Chapel of Golgotha, marks the tenth station.

15. The Chapel of the Nailing to the Cross, is at the eleventh station.

16. The Chapel of the Crucifixion is at the twelfth station.

17. At the thirteenth station is the Altar of Our Lady of Sorrows and a Chapel in honor of Saint Longinus, the Roman who oversaw the crucifixion - who later became a Christian.

18. At the fourteenth station is the Tomb of Christ and a Chapel in honor of Joseph Arimathea and Nicodemus.

19. The Orthodox Church of Saint Gabriel.

20. The Synagogue Church.

21. The Church of Saint Joseph.

22. The Church of Mount Carmel.

23. The Church on tip of Mount Nebo.

24. The Benedictine Monastery and chapel at Abu Ghosh.

A woman pilgrim to the Holy Land was coming to the end of her pilgrimage. She came with only one purpose: To find Jesus in the Holy Land, in someone, someplace, some event. In tears she concluded that she failed in finding Jesus, and was to go home the next day. As she boarded the bus to the airport, she was filled with an inexplicable joy. She found Jesus in the bus driver. She looked around – to find Jesus in her companions on the bus, on those walking the streets, on those sipping coffee at restaurants. She found Jesus everywhere. Her search for Jesus ended with her finding Jesus in everyone, through new eyes – true to the Lord's words: *"Truly, I say to you, as you did it to one of the least of them my brethren, you did it to me."* Mt.25:40

CHAPTER ELEVEN

Tourist Spots

"His rule will extend from sea to sea." Zachariah 9:10

Dead Sea: This is the lowest place on earth – 1388 feet below sea level – with half the territory in Jordan. It is 50 kilometers long and 15 kilometers wide, with no exit. Because there is no exit, and water only evaporates, it gets saltier, by the day. It is the saltiest sea – 8 times more than others. Therefore, it is called the Sea of Salt, Sea of Solitude, Asphalt Sea and Sea of Satan. It can support no life form - even fish. But because of its density, it can let people float in it. There are pictures of people floating and reading newspapers. And, of people finding healing – arthritis and psoriasis. A picture of the Dead Sea – sandy at first, turning to green, then to blue – appears below.

Earlier the Jordan River used to flow into it. Now, the river is diverted for agriculture, and the sea is drying up very fast. Very near the sea are the towns of Sodom and Gomorrah.

Red Sea: A ride in a glass-bottom boat on the Red Sea is a high point. The coral reefs and multi-colored fish are a delight to the eye. The Red Sea gets its name from the red hue it sports – caused by ferric and ferrous salts in the surrounding mountains. In the sun, the glint of red on the sea is a pleasure to watch.

Yad Vashen: The name is derived from Isaiah 56: 5. It is Israel's official memorial – located on Mount Remembrance - to six million Jewish Holocaust victims, who perished through Nazi persecution, which started in 1933. It consists of a complex of museums, outdoor monuments, exhibition halls, an archive, a library and other resource-centers. One avenue is lined with plaques of names of those who risked their lives for other Jews. It houses 68 million pages of documents, 300,000 photographs and thousands of films and videos on victims and survivors. An eternal flame burns in memory of the dead. Like the flame, memories are eternal.

Sharm-El-Sheikh: On our way to Cairo we halt at this popular resort. The place boasts of modern houses – clean and freshly painted – trimmed gardens, geometrically designed streets and a fine sea-front. It is a city carved out of sand-

The Dead Sea

"O Lord, our Lord, your greatness is seen in all the world."

Ps. 8: 1.

View of the Dead Sea through a glass bottom boat

"Lord, you have made many things! How wisely you have made them all!" Ps. 104: 24.

blown waste. No wonder that tourists from different parts of the world crowd here. Israel conquered this city in a war, but returned it to Egypt through a peace treaty.

Suez Canal: On our drive from Sharm-El-Sheikh to Cairo, we pass under the Suez Canal. The tunnel, under the sea, is about 1800 meters long. The sea above the tunnel is 300 meters wide and 28 meters deep. The canal itself is 190 kilometers, but the tunnel is a short passage under it. This engineering marvel was designed and built in the last part of the nineteenth century. Today it is an important waterway for international shipping. Recently we read of a huge container-loaded ship stuck in the canal, much to the grief of other ships whose passage was blocked. Thankfully, the blockage was cleared days later, to the relief of the shipping community.

The Pyramids and Sphinx: These are splendid tourist attractions. Three large pyramids and a few small ones are silent testimony to ancient architecture and resourcefulness. Standing below them we wonder how engineers of old planned and constructed these wonders, when tools and equipment were not sophisticated.

Built in honor of royalty, we are amazed at the extent to which they would go to keep alive the memory of their rulers. It is reported that each stone at the base of each pyramid weighed ten tons, and at higher levels of the monument each stone weighed two and a half tons. The stones were not hewn from nearby rocks, but from Aswan, in the South of Egypt. They were pushed on to barges on the Nile, that floated on the river to reach a point near the site of construction. They were then moved on skates to reach the site. Imagine the skill, effort, cost and time involved in the making of each pyramid; and there are many!

Each side of a big pyramid is 250 meters; the four sides equal a kilometre. Age has ravaged the monuments, but their sheer size and engineering excellence continue to amaze visitors. Close to the Pyramids is the Sphinx – a monument that couples man and animal – face of a man and body of a lion. The Pharaoh built it as a warning to reckless invaders – *'attack at your own peril'* – stemming from the boast of Egyptian arms and skilled soldiers.

"For God all things are possible." Mk. 10: 27.

The Egyptian Museum: Over a hundred thousand items are on display in this massive building. The reign of Pharaohs - over 5000 years – is on show. Ancient art and culture are deftly woven into the tapestry of the exhibits. We were in awe of their ingenuity and skill. The entry ticket appears below.

EGYPTIAN
MUSEUM
819052
G 75 L.E.

Author Page

Greetings!

I thank you for the interest you have shown in my book. If you liked what you read in MEETING JESUS IN THE HOLY LAND, please tell others. Please share your thoughts by way of a short review on Amazon. My website www.ignatiusfernandez.com hosts the link to the Amazon Page.

I thank you for your time and indulgence. God bless you and yours.

Ignatius Fernandez

He was in Industry for thirty years. Rising from the ranks he operated as General Manager, Director and Chief Executive. Later, he moved to academics to be Professor of Management in Business Schools and Corporate Trainer for senior managers. As speaker, counselor for families, blogger and author, he widened the band width of his profile.

http://www.facebook.com/ignatius.fernandez.3
https://www.linkedin.com/in/
ignatiusfernandez-56874645?trk=hp-identity-photo
https://twitter.com/ignatius1939
https://www.pinterest.com/fernandez0709/
http://thechildisfatheroftheman.blogspot.in/

Twelve books by the author:
* Meeting JESUS in the Holy Land
* JESUS CHRIST Peerless Leader
* Jesus Christ Teaches and Trains Today's Managers
* Think Christ, Live Christian
* Jesus Christ – True Leader and Perfect Gentleman

* The Child is Father of the Man – Tips and Techniques for Wise Parenting

* The Golden Rule – For Empowering Professional Relationships

* The Heart has its Reasons – Looking Back Looking Ahead

* Life Lessons – A Christian Sharing

* Through the Eye of a Needle – Transforming Relationships

* Relationship Management – The Master's Way

* My Family – The Next Best Thing That Happened to Me

And, over sixty of his articles appear in magazines, on international websites and blogs